Gift or a Given?

A Theology of Healing for the
Twenty-first Century

Gift or a Given?

A Theology of Healing for the
Twenty-first Century

John P. Atkinson

Winchester, UK
Washington, USA

First published by Circle Books, 2012
Circle Books is an imprint of John Hunt Publishing Ltd., Laurel House, Station Approach,
Alresford, Hants, SO24 9JH, UK
office1@o-books.net
www.o-books.com

For distributor details and how to order please visit the 'Ordering' section on our website.

Text copyright: John P. Atkinson 2011

ISBN: 978 1 78099 426 0

A CIP catalogue record for this book is available from the British Library.

Design: Lee Nash

Printed in the USA by Edwards Brothers Malloy

We operate a distinctive and ethical publishing philosophy in all
areas of our business, from our global network of authors to
production and worldwide distribution.

CONTENTS

To the memory of
the Rev'd Dr Angela Shier-Jones, (1960-2011)
theologian, pastor, healer and good friend, without whose
example and insight this whole account would never
have happened

Preface

When I was training at Hartley Victoria College, Manchester in the early 1980s my tutor used to talk about a lack of theological reflection in my project work. Only after some persistence in the last few weeks of study did we, as a student group, get him to explain precisely what he meant by this term "theological reflection". It boiled down to the fact that we have to allow our practical experience and our knowledge of Bible and doctrine to react dynamically to make sense of faith and the world.

I have to admit that it still took a few years in practical ministry before this really became real to me. This book is the result of precisely that process. I have been active in the ministry of healing for at least twenty-five years, have experienced different circumstances and outcomes and have also gradually broadened out my view as to what this ministry entails.

In the chapters that follow I have first of all tried to set out the personal journey of practice in and around the ministry of healing which has led to the reflections I share. As I have talked with friends and colleagues about this I get the impression that what I am offering is a different perspective. I hope that it will at the very least provoke the reader to further theological reflection.

In the course of preparation I sought comments from friends and was asked by one whether I was going to give examples of other people's healing ministries. I have generally restricted my examples to those which I (or, in a couple of instances, my wife) have experienced at first hand. In a sense these are the experiences upon which I can most fruitfully reflect.

Introduction

I can trace my interest in the ministry of healing back to the 1970s when, as an active lay person, I was invited by my then minister, Eric Challoner, to join him with one or two others to pray for specific people with need for healing. We shared on two occasions and I would judge that each of the people concerned experienced what they would have described as "healing" — one physical and one spiritual. I will not go into details at this point because the cases are not particularly relevant to what follows.

Having been accepted for training for the Methodist Presbyteral Ministry in 1981 I was somewhat preoccupied with academic and practical study and it was not until I found myself preaching on the topic of "Christ the Healer" that I gave healing within the church much thought. Being a visiting preacher it was essentially a matter of raising the question of whether the church engages in a healing ministry and then leaving the congregation to think about it. I doubt whether they did

A couple of years later I was in pastoral charge of a local church when the topic came round again. On this occasion I felt challenged that if no-one else was going to do anything, I, at least, as the minister ought to take responsibility. It was a communion service and having preached on healing I invited anyone who wished to receive the laying-on of hands to remain kneeling at the communion rail after receiving the elements. One man remained behind. When I asked if he had any particular concern he indicated that it wasn't really "healing" he wanted but a blessing as he was starting a new job the next day. After the service, as I was shaking hands with the congregation, one of the women was obviously tearful. When I enquired if there was something wrong she said that she had been suffering for thirty years and in all that time she had never heard a suggestion that the church had anything to offer her. (In that time she had attended churches of different denominations and had done so regularly.) Whether the offer had never explicitly been made or whether she had simply not heard it, I cannot say; but it was certainly a challenge to me.

I arranged to visit her and her husband within a couple of days. This was a middle aged woman who, it transpired, had suffered a form of agoraphobia for thirty years, having had a panic attack in a shop when her daughter was five years old. With her husband's support she had managed to pursue a career as an office worker. Her boss would pick her up from home and drop her back in the evening. She could only go shopping if accompanied by her husband. Life was really quite restricted.

I prayed with them in the home and, I think, I laid hands on her head. There was no dramatic instantaneous healing but two things happened. Firstly her daughter, who despite living next door to her mother knew nothing of her health problems, came into the house and asked what had happened — 'The house feels different'. Secondly she went to her GP who referred her to a Psychiatrist who in turn organised a Psychiatric Social Worker for her. Through medication and supportive therapy together with regular prayer in the home, she was eventually restored to a proper degree of health. This early experience shows how healing is a process rather than an event. The irony in this case was that the husband, who had effectively carried his wife for thirty years, suffered a nervous breakdown when she appeared no longer to need him. Thankfully that was dealt with through the normal medical channels. Healing can sometimes be disruptive!

At about that time I got to know a couple who had been engaged in healing ministry outside the mainline church for some years. They had joined the Methodist Church following a marriage which I had conducted. The young woman in particular had gifts of insight and of healing which were quite special. I invited them to share with me within the church pastoral setting.

We, four of us including my wife, would visit members in their homes offering prayer with the laying on of hands. The cases were varied and so therefore were the results: a woman suffering in bereavement finding reassurance; an elderly woman in need of a hip replacement but with a weak heart supported until she was well enough to have the operation; a young woman with endometriosis who had been told she would never have children and would not be allowed to adopt because her husband was too old. As I wrote the first draft of this paragraph, the latter's son celebrated his 21st birthday!

Eventually the number of calls was becoming unsustainable so we agreed to hold a weekly service of healing in a small country chapel inviting people to attend if they could; taking them if they needed transport, or remembering them in prayer if they were unable to attend.

The format comprised a short opening time of worship followed by sharing of concerns and then individuals were invited to come and sit on one of two chairs at the front. Here one or sometimes two would place hands on the head of the person concerned or over the particular source of pain, if appropriate.

This carried on for several years on a weekly basis. When I left Newport and moved to Swansea I introduced a similar pattern there. In 1994 we moved to work in Berlin, Germany. In the course of the first twelve months there I interested my German colleague in the topic of healing and following a series of bilingual Bible studies we offered weekly prayers. These started in 1996 and are, to my knowledge, still taking place in 2011, though no doubt with a slight variation in pattern.

I was interested to discover that the German Methodist Church (Evangelisch-methodistische Kirche or EmK) was very reticent about the healing ministry. Having asked the Bishop whether it might be helpful to call together interested parties to discuss the topic I received the comment that they had held a theological conversation that had produced nothing—'perhaps someone ought to do something practical and report on it'. This my colleague and I duly did in a report to the North German Annual Conference in 1997. This included a number of testimonies from individuals who had benefited from healing prayer. At the Annual Conference of 2000 we presented a proposed German translation of *Prayers and Ideas for Healing Services* by Ian Cowie (© 1995 Wild Goose Publications) for the use of the EmK. In that year I was invited to address seminars on healing at the World Methodist Conference at Brighton. I was also asked to address seminars at the Spiritual Renewal conferences in Braunfels, Germany, attended by members from German, Austrian, Swiss and other European EmK jurisdictions. It was interesting to discover that the German-speaking "charismatics" were also reticent about healing ministry, requiring it to be very carefully ordered.

When I returned to Britain in 2002 I was invited to succeed Jim Needham as the Methodist Connexional Advisor for Health and Healing, a post which I still hold in 2011.

Whilst in Berlin we had befriended a young couple from the United States who had become interested in healing whilst with us. Subsequently we maintained contact, and this led to a broadening of my perspective. I was told of a conference held at my friends' church for "Parish Nurses" which had concluded with a service of healing. At the World Methodist Conference in 2000 I had met one or two women who had described themselves as Parish Nurses but I had not really understood what this meant.

As I was due for a sabbatical in 2003 I decided to investigate what Parish Nursing actually was. I visited Holland, Michigan, in the United States, a relatively small town and discovered that there were a number of Parish Nurses ministering there. Most of these were nominally employed by the local hospital board but paid by church congregations. The one in my friends' church was half-time and employed by the congregation of this Lutheran church. I will write more about Parish Nursing in a later chapter.

However, as part of this investigation I read *Alive and Kicking* by Stephen Pattison. This was a book which I had declined to read in when it was passed to me in 1990 because I felt it undermined my focus on the ministry of healing, but now its time had clearly come!

What struck me about this book was Pattison's observation that the church seems to focus healing ministry upon asking God to intervene and make people well when it might be a better priority to engage in preventing them becoming ill in the first place! (I grossly simplify here and apologise to Stephen Pattison for doing so but it was this aspect that spoke to me at the time.)

Parish Nurses whom I visited were engaged in, for instance, health education, pastoral visiting, promoting donation of bone marrow, organising advice on medicines. I had gone to the United States anticipating that an American model would not cross the Atlantic but returned convinced that this was a significant aspect of pastoral care which could well be developed in the United Kingdom.

Since then I have been seeking to promote this ministry including a pilot project in Lichfield Methodist Church. (See chapter 7.)

Meanwhile my own healing ministry has continued and I owe it to the reader to describe my personal practice and the way it has developed.

As noted above I initially offered laying-on of hands at the communion rail and then in the home and did so with a short prayer. Having come into contact with friends experienced in healing ministry I became aware of what is sometimes referred to as "hot hands". When I asked how one discovered this gift my friend simply advised me to place my hands near to each other and see if I could feel anything. The answer was in the negative.

However, later I went to join my wife, who had gone to bed suffering with a headache. She appeared to be asleep so out of curiosity I held by hand over her head. When she opened her eyes I was a little embarrassed but she informed me that when I'd put my hand over her forehead the headache had gone. I was somewhat shocked. This did seem to suggest that there was more involved here than "simply" asking God to take pain away.

I was a part-time hospital chaplain at the time and found that this ability (gift?) was helpful on occasion in reducing patients' pain. I think of the husband of a church member whom I happened to visit on my rounds who was in severe discomfort with gall stones. While I sat and talked to him on his bed I placed my hand on his lower back, where the pain was. This seemed to ease the pain at the time. Some days later I received a call from his wife telling me that he had been amazed how the pain had gone. He was not a church member or a believer and I don't recall that I spoke a prayer with him, though I may have done.

Looking back with hindsight I would now wonder about the propriety of this sort of "freelance, unsupervised" ministry in a hospital setting but there is no doubt that benefit was received. I intend to refer later to a programme broadcast in Germany in 2011 which described the formal interaction in some German hospitals between scientific medicine and alternative therapies.

I would add at this juncture that since there was no place for healing in the training syllabus in College I have always been learning by experience and have no doubt on occasion crossed some lines which might have been better left uncrossed. It remains a concern to me that there is almost no coverage of the topic of healing in our current ordination training packages or, if there is, it is at a very superficial level.

Over the years, despite the fact that for most of that time I was sharing in the leadership of regular healing services, I have come to the conclusion that healing should neither be confined to liturgical settings nor necessarily placed within a recognised prayer format. This is not to imply that there is no place for a formal liturgical setting. For seven years my appointment permitted only one healing service per month and that within the context of

Communion. This does raise issues which will be discussed later about the attitude of the Church to healing. The style of healing prayer offered tends to relate to the tradition of the church concerned or that of the practitioner. If you see a special sacramental focus in the Eucharist it may seem to be the uniquely appropriate point for offering healing. If you have a less eucharistically based ministry it will almost certainly be in another setting.

Again, practice over the years has led me to demur from verbalising specific healing prayer requests unless it seems to be pastorally helpful to the recipient. I cite two illustrations, though I could offer more: A member of the congregation was obviously in some discomfort after a Sunday service. My enquiry elicited the response that she had back pain. I invited her to come round to the house later on, which she did. I placed my hands on her shoulders and back anticipating a reduction in the pain. A day or so later I enquired about her condition and was informed that though she still had back pain her asthma had cleared completely. (Some years later I witnessed her recounting this to someone else and she confirmed that until that day she had had quite severe asthma often necessitating time off work. Since then she had had only mild attacks and hadn't missed a day.) My spoken prayer would have been for her back but the healing came to her breathing.

A second example: a musician friend had blocked sinuses so I placed my hands around her head. The sinuses quickly cleared. The next day the sinuses were blocked again but a shoulder injury which she had had for years and which was a particular problem for a viola player had been healed completely. She has never had a recurrence of this problem despite subsequently becoming a full-time orchestral player. Again neither she nor I had any thought of the shoulder injury as I ministered to her.

One theological comment might be that God knows better what is needed and will respond as necessary without direction from any agent. But, as may become clear later in the book, there are other ways of considering the healing process which remove the necessity of explaining the apparent vagaries of divine intervention and misconceptions about why some people are "not healed".

Another perspective that bears thinking about is the uniqueness of Christian healing—healing in the name of Christ. Some Christian healers maintain that unless healing is offered in the name of Jesus it will not work, or, if it appears to do so, it is a counterfeit and will later revert. It seems to me that this is blinkered. Although I personally consider that any care I offer as a Christian derives from my commitment to the Risen Christ, it is nevertheless clear to me that genuine healing occurs within most religious traditions and that similar results can also be achieved by people of no formal belief. To suggest that this is "demonic counterfeit" seems to go counter to the genuine benefit which some people receive. It is worth adding that others of ill will can use healing as a means of manipulating vulnerable people. Where there are positive gifts they can always be abused. I will reflect later on our relationship to other faiths.

In recent years I have spent a good deal of time engaged in the growing activities of Churches Together for Healing, a co-ordinating group of Churches Together in England which seeks to promote the ministry of healing within the main denominations. Sharing in discussion with colleagues from other churches can be quite liberating as you come to see things through someone else's eyes. At one such regional meeting a United Reformed colleague commented that in his church they no longer have "intercessions" but only "prayers for healing"—healing of the nations, healing of society, healing of the church, healing of individuals. I shall reflect on the nature of healing, wholeness and salvation later in the book.

One significant point worth making is the weight of words and the import of their meaning. In Berlin there were two evangelically minded ministers. One was charismatic and the other was not. The first held "prayers for healing" the other insisted on calling them "prayers for the sick". A friend who had come out of the Spiritualist movement would speak of "clairvoyance" whereas the same ability in the charismatic context would almost certainly be categorised as "gift of discernment" or "gift of prophecy" depending on the form it took. We have to be very careful in using words. We have to define carefully what we mean by "healing". Howard Booth wrote a very helpful book *Healing is Wholeness* (sadly long out of print) which makes this point. Many people have been put off healing ministry because of perceived failure to 'get better'. One of the most moving experiences of the earlier years of my engagement with the healing ministry was ministering to a man with terminal stomach cancer who—incidentally, having been recommended to do so by his Catholic priest— came weekly to our healing services. After he died, his wife continued coming to the services for some months because "they did Dave so much good". Death is not necessarily defeat, though the expression "Death is the ultimate healer" tends to be a little trite.

Another concern I have is that healing is a ministry of the whole Church not just individual members. If the ministry ceases when a minister leaves, then the Church has failed to own it. This happened when I left one church—for which I therefore acknowledge some responsibility—but having learned from that I made sure at the next one that a team was empowered to carry on. I will discuss this later on.

Beyond this I have found myself reflecting on what is physically happening when healing takes place. I wrote earlier of having "hot hands". One reasonably sceptical friend submitted to the "hands treatment" after we had spent a day in a conference hall and his knee was painful. As I held my hand above his knee he remarked "It must be microwaves!" (He was a former chemistry teacher). It seems to me that we have to think rationally about the possibility that this is not miraculous inter-vention but some form of direction of natural energies. Alongside that, one has also to reflect on how healing can be transmitted down a phone line, as has on at least one occasion happened in my case. No doubt one can speak of psychological effects but we also have to make sense of incidents when we seem to have intuitive links to relatives who live at a distance—the "That's funny I was about to phone you!" sort of thing.

To what extent is healing "tapping into" the natural processes of the world? Does this give a different perspective on working with God? More later.

I hope this introduction at least gives an insight into the way my own thinking has progressed and brought me to this point. I hope too that you can stay with me in my journey of exploration.

I intend to examine how healing is portrayed in the Old and New Testament and how thinking and practice have developed over church history, in an attempt to contextualise the image of healing that is given and to understand how this influences the way we exercise ministry today. I hope to challenge the perception that healing is a concern of a (charismatic?) minority in the Christian community and to encourage the Church to recognise it as a central priority of the Gospel.

Chapter I

What's in a Name?

I was no linguist at school, though I did manage to pass what was then known as GCE Ordinary Level French. Only when my wife and I made friends with an Austrian family did I become interested in foreign languages and in particular in German. Working in Germany, albeit predominantly with English-speaking people, it became essential to acquire a decent competence in German and I did learn enough to be able to read it fairly comfortably.

Using a different language sometimes sparks new ways of thinking about words and therefore about the concepts, in this case theological concepts, that relate to them. As an example the German word *Gerechtigkeit"* is usually translated as "righteousness". In English we tend to think of righteousness in terms of good behaviour or "moral rectitude". In German it is linked with the sense of fairness and justice. It relates to being acquitted—declared innocent. Hence it is also translated as "justification". To be righteous is to be justified. The difference can make a subtle difference to how you interpret biblical teaching.

Similarly I have been fascinated by the relationship between a number of theological words with a shared root which cast light on what we mean by "healing". There is a similar relationship in Greek. These German words share the root *heil*. Related to this is the difference in meaning between "curing" and "healing" which sometimes causes misunderstandings in the area of healing ministry and people's expectations.

Unfortunately most English-speakers, even if they have no knowledge of German will be familiar with the cry "Heil Hitler!"

We recognise it as a shout of approbation for the Nazi dictator. We probably don't make the connection with "Hail Caesar!" or "Hail! King of the Jews!" It is equivalent to "God save the Queen". It is a greeting wishing health and success. It can also mean "salvation".

But here are some other words with the same root *heil*:

heilen	to heal/cure
Heiler	healer
Heiland	Saviour
heilsam	healthy
heilig	holy
heiligkeit	holiness

This German root also links with the English word "whole" and therefore with ideas of perfection and completion. This is confirmed by the range of meanings of the Greek words σωξω (sozo): heal, recover, save, whole; and σωτήρια (soteria): health, safety, salvation, saving.

A German friend told me that a child whose doll's arm had come off might ask her father to heal it (*heilen/heil machen*) in the sense of "put it back together".

That said, one can begin to get the sense that when we talk of healing we are using a potentially loaded term and one not to be used lightly.

In "Healing in the New Testament" John J Pilch offers some insights from medical anthropology to which I shall refer in the next chapter, but he also offers some helpful definitions. He suggests that we should differentiate between disease and illness, the former being a scientifically verifiable condition and the latter a state of being. By this definition Pilch notes (p153) 'Curing is the strategy of destroying or checking a pathogen, removing a malfunctioning or non-functioning organ, restoring a person to health or well-being.' (He adds: 'It occurs rarely'.)

In contrast (p155) "in medical anthropology, healing is the restoration of meaning to life. It is the strategy of restoring social and personal meaning for life problems that accompany human health misfortunes".

I suspect that not everyone will accept these definitions but they do seem to me to relate to the proposal that "healing is wholeness".

Returning to the various definitions in Greek and German we can begin to see how the concepts of healing and salvation relate; that "the Lord our Saviour" can be understood as synonymous with "the Lord our Healer". Going beyond Greek to the Hebrew of the Old Testament consider Jeremiah 17:14 "Heal me, O LORD, and I shall be healed; save me, and I shall be saved"; the point is nicely confirmed by the Hebrew poetic parallelism of the prophetic words.

Following on from this line of thought we may also be able to recognise the possibility of healing the Creation, or of salvation being expressed through the healing of relationships, or even of institutions.

It has seemed to me for a long time that it is possible to be suffering from a physical and/or mental condition which might be perceived as a disability and yet be a "whole", balanced and fulfilled person. In contrast it is also possible to be physically fit and apparently mentally sound and yet not be "whole" in the same sense.

When we come to look at the way healing is portrayed or interpreted in scripture and through the history of the Christian community, it will always be important to hold these thoughts in mind.

Chapter 2

Biblical Focus

In this chapter I wish to explore the way in which healing is described in the Old and New Testaments and to attempt to consider it within its cultural setting. In other words, to look at examples from the texts and to understand the world view of the authors and of the people whom they describe. For example, if you consider that illness is the consequence of sin, then that will alter the way you offer healing. If you believe that incapacity is given by a God whose will is not to be questioned, or that pain is given for the purpose of personal growth, it will affect the way you tell the story and in due course how it will be interpreted.

2.1 Old Testament

Whether you are inclined to interpret the first chapters of Genesis literally or not it is clear that theologically we are to understand that the physical universe was the result of a creative act and it was originally created good. The inability of human beings to live in harmony with that created order is said to be the cause of all that is dysfunctional in our present world. Disobedience has at various points, according to the biblical authors, led to disasters either natural, such as the Flood, or more often political such as the exile in Babylon. A healthy society according to the prophets is one in which the powerless and vulnerable are protected. In Isaiah 58:7-8 there is an interesting statement to this effect: "Is it not sharing your food with the hungry, taking the homeless poor into your house, clothing the naked when you meet them, and never evading a duty to your kinsfolk? Then your light will break forth like the dawn, and *new skin will speedily grow over your wound...*" This last clause reads "thine health shall spring forth speedily" in the Authorised Version. Either way the implication is that health will be found within a just and caring society.

Within that wider context we nevertheless see examples of specific healing within the Old Testament, several of these associated with Elisha.

In 2 Kings 4, a Shunammite woman who had been generous to Elisha became pregnant having given up hope of a child. Later this child injured his head and Elisha was summoned to help. In the short term his staff, which had spiritual power, was laid upon the child, but eventually when Elisha arrived he lay upon the child, breathed into his mouth and shared bodily warmth. The child then recovered. The modern reader is bound to wonder whether the child was in a kind of coma induced by severe concussion. Elisha's action sounds remarkably like a combination of mouth to mouth resuscitation and very full laying on of "hands" (of "body", more accurately).

There are numerous laws in Leviticus dealing with so-called leprosy (which certainly was not what we call leprosy today). 2 Kings 5 tells the story of Naaman who was healed of leprosy at Elisha's direction by bathing in the Jordan.

On the other hand there are cases where healing is declined. In 2 Kings 1:2, Ahaziah fell from the roof and was injured. Worried if he would survive he asked for a prognosis from the god Ekron but the messengers were intercepted by Elisha who said that because of his faithlessness to God he would not recover. This contrasts with the story of Naaman who was seeking healing from the prophet of the Lord.

It is notable that in the Old Testament the Lord is the source of disease as well as the source of healing.

In Deuteronomy 28, among the curses that will befall Israel if they do not choose to follow that Lord are: (v27-28) "May the Lord strike you with Egyptian boils and with tumours, scabs, and itch, for which you will find no cure. May the Lord strike you with madness, blindness and stupefaction."

In 2 Chronicles 16, "Asa became gravely affected with disease in his feet; he did not seek guidance of the Lord but resorted to physicians." (He died two years later!) One hesitates to draw a conclusion about the relation of faith and reference to physicians in modern society!

In 2 Chronicles 21:18-19, "After this the Lord struck down the king (Joram) with an incurable disease of the bowels. It continued for some time, and towards the end of the second year the disease caused his bowels to prolapse, and the painful ulceration brought on his death."

In Hosea 5:13 the prophet uses sickness figuratively but if health is to be perceived in a wider sense and applicable to whole societies the example is appropriate: "When Ephraim found that he was sick, and Judah was covered with sores, Ephraim turned to Assyria and sent envoys to the Great King. But he had no power to cure you or heal your sores"

A few verses later in Hosea 6:1, we find: "Come let us return to the Lord. He has torn us, but he will heal us, he has wounded us, but he will bind up our wounds."

Clearly, here is an active interventionist God who uses people's health and sickness as a means to make points about spiritual discipline and obedience. We find this understanding in the mind of Jesus' contemporaries: "Who sinned, this man or his parents...?" (see below)

Another story, which finds an echo in John's Gospel (3:14), is that of the bronze serpent in Numbers 21. The Israelites 'grew impatient and spoke against God and Moses' (v4-5) and in consequence the Lord sent a plague of venomous snakes. When the people repented the Lord directed Moses to make a bronze snake and erect it on a pole. 'Anyone bitten by a snake could look at the bronze serpent and recover' (v9). This use of the serpent is in itself interesting since it relates to various traditions in other cultures and in particular remains in modern medicine as a symbol of healing: the image outside some surgeries and pharmacies.

Elijah, who was Elisha's mentor found himself in need of healing in 1 Kings 19. I have heard it suggested that the story of Elijah's flight after defeating the prophets of Baal shows all the symptoms of a nervous breakdown. After the dramatic showdown on Mount Carmel, Elijah suddenly panicked and ran away. "It is enough!" he is recorded as saying. He wanted to die. He journeyed for forty days and nights to Mount Horeb. He kept protesting to God that he was the only one left and that he was unworthy. A sense of isolation and uselessness are common features of depression. The God who had shown himself in power on Carmel finally revealed himself to Elijah in a still small voice: "Why are you here Elijah?" There follows what might well be interpreted as a short session of 'talking therapy' along with encouragement to carry on.

In the account of the relationship between Saul and David in 1 Samuel we find the use of 'music therapy' as a means to calm Saul's mental condition—or to overcome the evil spirit that overwhelmed him. Saul's behaviour, though his suspicion was not totally unwarranted since David had already been anointed as his successor, appears to indicate paranoia and mood swings. David played his harp to quieten Saul's mind. I heard recently that today the harp is again being used to similar beneficial effect.

As distinct from the narrative accounts it is clearly the case that the authors of the Psalms and the Prophets assumed that God had the power to heal. Some verses plead for God's intervention (Psalm 6:2, 41:4); others thank God that they have been healed (Psalm 30:2) whilst others describe God's healing (Psalm 107:20, 147:3).

Bearing in mind the reference to mental health in the instances of Elijah and Saul above, it would appear that in some of the Psalmists' verses the writer or the subject of the Psalm is suffering or has suffered from depression, be it psychological or spiritual.

Psalm 40:2 is often used in this context: "he raised me out of the miry pit, out of the mud and clay; he set my feet on rock and gave me a firm footing". If might be argued that this could relate to other circumstances of difficulty but the implication is the same. God is the one who heals and/or restores—God is the one who saves.

One cannot leave this section without referring to redemptive suffering, as in Isaiah 53:5. "The chastisement he bore restored us to health and by his wounds we are healed". Whether or not that is to be understood to be a prophecy about Jesus, it is nevertheless a profound truth that healing cannot simply be offered or received without significant cost to those involved, especially when healing is needed at an institutional level.

2.2 New Testament

When we contemplate the place of healing in the modern church and then read through the Gospels, Acts and the Epistles it is hard to come to terms with the changed perspective. The number of times that Jesus himself offered healing was such that it was seen to be a central part of his ministry. When he sent his disciples out on mission he told them to share the good news and to heal. When Paul was on his missionary journeys he also healed people and found himself in consequence at the centre of unwanted attention.

Jesus healed the blind, people with skin diseases, Peter's mother who had a fever, the woman who had a long-term problem with haemorrhaging. He brought back to life people who had been pronounced dead. He also healed people with what we might today principally term psychiatric conditions but who then were thought to be possessed of demons. I do not wish to go into detail in terms of textual references; other writers have done so eloquently and the New Testament stands ready for the reader to investigate if he or she has any doubts.

However I mentioned above "Healing in the New Testament"

by John J Pilch who addresses the New Testament record from the perspective of medical anthropology. It is quite normal I think for modern readers to approach the healing stories from a perspective that assumes contemporary medical knowledge and therefore to overlook the fact that the First Century world view was quite different.

Pilch's analysis is far too complicated for this book to deal with but, as an example, he contrasts the difference between modern Western (specifically USA) health perspectives and those of the First Century. Whereas 'Western scientific (medicine has an) emphasis on doing, individualism, and human nature as neutral or good...the New Testament idea of health emphasises:

- being and/or becoming (that is states), not doing (activity)
- collateral and linear relationships not individualism
- present and past time orientation, not the future
- the uncontrollable factor of nature, not its manipulation or mastery
- human nature as both good and bad, not neutral and correctable.'

He summarises: 'The sickness problems presented to Jesus in the New Testament are concerned with a state of being (blind; deaf; mute; leprosy; death; uncontrolled haemorrhaging...) rather than an inability to function'.

Pilch, not surprisingly, has many other insights which merit close reading. He examines leprosy in detail, making the point that it does not refer to modern leprosy (Hansen's Disease) but more likely to conditions such as psoriasis or eczema. And the consequence of the illness was social exclusion. He looks at the Gospel writers and examines their particular perspectives and cultural settings which would inevitably lead to varied presentations of sickness and healing. He draws, for instance, a comparison between Luke's and Mark's respective descriptions of the condition of Peter's mother-in-law. Mark says she was suffering from a fever; Luke says she was possessed by a spirit called Fever. In Mark Jesus took her by the hand and she got up while Luke says Jesus cast out the demon. One can presumably draw the conclusion that the medical understandings of the two authors' communities were different. We can reasonably conclude, I think, that it is at the very least unwise to draw too specific conclusions from the circumstances described.

It is clear from the Gospel accounts that Jesus' contemporaries considered illness or disability to be a consequence of sin. Bearing in mind the accounts in the Old Testament that is hardly surprising. In truth we all try to find reasons for suffering and usually want to lay blame somewhere else. In that sense little has changed over the centuries. So, as I alluded to above, the question asked of Jesus when he met the blind man (John 9) was whether it was the man's own fault or his parents' that he had been born blind. One can surmise that this was probably a matter of debate amongst the religious scholars as well as the common people. Nevertheless Jesus denied that it had anything to do with the man's sins or those of his parents. On the other hand, the implication that he was born blind so that Jesus could eventually heal him is not much of an encouragement to the modern reader!

In a similar vein, the man let down through the roof in Mark 2:1-12 was both forgiven his sins and healed of his lameness. This again led to debate about whether Jesus had authority to forgive sins. (One wonders whether the religious authorities considered Psalm 103:3 "He pardons all my wrongdoing and heals all my ills" — or indeed whether the gospel writer had that verse in mind.)

In truth it is almost certainly the case that in approaching healing we are bound to take into account the world view of the people concerned. If they believe their condition is connected with sin, then it is appropriate to release them from it. If they believe that they have been cursed by someone it is probably appropriate to free them from the curse.

Pilch also draws attention to the way in which the body and its functions were perceived in the First Century and before. The eyes and the heart were linked—heart for thinking, eyes for collecting information; the mouth and the ears—for communicating and receiving communication; the hands and feet—for acting or behaving. They knew nothing of the function of the brain.

I think most of us are aware that the understanding of the reproductive system was also completely different. Nothing was known of the interaction of sperm and egg. It was thought that the man planted a seed in the woman. She simply carried his child. One can reflect on the implications of this for the doctrine of the Virgin Birth and it is also a useful commentary on John 1:13 'who were born, not of blood, nor of the will of the flesh, nor of the will of man, but of God'

Notwithstanding these caveats about what was understood of the human body and its health, it is still undeniable that healing played a significant part in the life of the first generations of Christians. Luke reports events in Acts and Paul refers to healing in his letters especially in the context of the gifts of the Spirit in 1 Corinthians.

2.3 The Pauline Perspective

There can, I believe, be little doubt that the attitude of the Christian community today towards healing is significantly influenced by the Pauline reference to the gifts of the Spirit. Most usual is reference to 1 Corinthians 12:9 listing healing (or "healings") among the gifts of the Spirit, confirmed a few verses later in Paul's listing in verse 28. Surprisingly (to me at least) Paul fails to mention healing when he refers to spiritual gifts in Romans 12:6-8 nor does he do so in Ephesians 4:11.

Within the Pentecostal movements of the last two centuries there seems to have been an emphasis on the individual gifts of the Spirit in their differentiated appearance. This may be a reflection on the increasingly individualistic nature of faith and Christian experience, springing from the personal experience of salvation which was so much the characteristic of the Evangelical Revival. Paul does indeed suggest that some people have one gift and others another but his ideal appears to be that all would experience everything.

When he speaks of the gifts he links them with the well-being of the whole church, with the mutual interdependence of the different members of the church community. It seems to me that it is rightly expressed in the terms that the gifts are available to the community and that some may be more "gifted" than others. Nevertheless they are communal rather than individual gifts. This will be reflected in a later topic, but I would want to express it thus: if a particularly "gifted" person happens not to be present when that "gift" is required it can be offered through other members of the community. Experience seems to confirm this to be the case.

For me this is a very important point insofar as I shall want to suggest that this focus on "healing ministry", and especially on charismatic healers, is one factor that leads to a whole can of worms which is opened when healing "doesn't work".

2.4 James

It is necessary to refer to James 5:14-15 which gives an insight into the practice of at least one part of the early Christian community. In this context the sick person is to request a visit from the "elders of the church" who will come, presumably as a group, to pray with the sick person using anointing with oil and doing so in the name of the Lord: 'the prayer offered in faith will heal the sick man, the Lord will restore him to health, and if he has committed sins they will be forgiven.' The key elements here seem to me to be the request—a desire for healing— the corporate response—rather than a designated individual— and restoration by "the Lord". (It is not clear whether "the Lord" means God or Jesus in this case.)

2.5 Conclusion

Sickness and healing are present in the whole of the Bible, though not as a major emphasis except in the ministry of Jesus and in the experience of the Early Church as described in Acts by Luke who was a recognised physician. In the Old Testament illness can be seen as punishment by God for inappropriate behaviour, and especially for turning away from the Lord.

In the Gospels healing is one of the signs of the presence of the coming Kingdom of God and is a fulfilment of the prophecy of Isaiah quoted by Jesus in Luke 4:18: 'he has sent me to announce good news to the poor, to proclaim release for prisoners and recovery of sight for the blind; to let the broken victims go free.' That healing was characterised principally by those benefiting being restored to full membership of their community. Through their healing they became whole again.

I cannot finish this chapter without reference to Revelation 22:2 which pictures the New Jerusalem, in the centre of which will be a tree whose leaves will bring healing to the nations. How much more central can healing be, and is it not significant that that healing is "for the nations"?

Chapter 3

What happened to healing?

It is obvious to anyone that the characteristics of the early Christian community were far removed from what we experience in the contemporary church, except in what appear to us to be exceptional circumstances. The Pentecostal Movement which originated in the 19th Century and some of the newly planted churches in the developing world can certainly exhibit patterns and similarities; in fact it is a regular feature of revival movements that they seek to rediscover the New Testament pattern of faith and community. But for the majority of the traditional churches the ministry of healing has either been institutionalised or marginalised, whereas, as we have seen, it was central to the ministry of Jesus and the apostles.

Over the years different explanations have been offered including the theological one that the gifts of the Spirit were given only for the Apostolic Age and were then withdrawn, to be focussed in the Church. There are other less theological reasons—though it has to be said, almost every division or trend in the church has some sort of theological basis, however obtuse (!).

In the New Testament we see an early example of the transition from charismatic freedom to institutional structure. Once the personal leadership of the Apostles becomes impossible it is replaced by appointments of bishops, presbyters, and deacons who have the responsibility for maintaining the apostolic tradition. Structure and discipline naturally restrict the freedom of the community to exercise what have earlier been recognised as communal gifts. So one can imagine that as the Church became increasingly clericalised and as it concurrently became associated with the Roman state the participation of the non-ordained would gradually be reduced in an effort to promote uniformity.

The early centuries were characterised by theological disputes and the identification of some of the dissidents as heretics. If you didn't agree with the judgement of the orthodox hierarchy you were excluded and your contribution usually rejected. The "laity" were reduced to participant observers in the liturgy and in parallel with the recognition of the Church as the spiritual arm of the state, membership of the church was also seen in terms of obedient citizenship and certainly not "democratic" (nor of course charismatic).

Not surprisingly, the practice of healing will be seen to have been focussed in formal aspects of the liturgy whilst in all likelihood still being present, though largely unrecorded, in the informality of pastoral care. Pastoral care, be it by an ordained person or by a member of the community out of compassion, is a key aspect of the healing ministry of the church, though often not recognised explicitly as such. One can of course only surmise, because there is very little written source material from which to draw clear facts.

In the year 263 CE Dionysius the Great, Bishop of Alexandria, sent an Easter Encyclical which included the following: "The present time," he writes, "does not appear a fit season for a festival … All things are filled with tears, all are mourning, and on account of the multitudes already dead and still dying, groans are daily heard throughout the city … There is not a house in which there is not one dead … After this, war and famine succeeded which we endured with the heathen, but we bore alone those miseries with which they afflicted us … But we rejoiced in the peace of Christ which he gave to us alone … *Most of our brethren by their exceeding great love and affection not sparing themselves and adhering to one another, were constantly superintending the sick, ministering to their wants without fear and cessation, and healing them in Christ."* The heathen, on the contrary, repelled the sick or cast them half-dead into the street.

Cyprian, Bishop of Carthage, tells us of the same self-denying charity in contrast to heathen selfishness manifested in Carthage during the raging of a pestilence, under the persecuting reign of Gallus (252CE)

Clearly at this point in the mid-third century there was community care and solidarity within the Christian community which was recognised as being different from the standards of the heathen (would we say secular?) society in which they were set.

As time goes on we need to be aware of the two streams of healing, one which seems to drift into the territory of the miraculous and the other which is secularised and generally unrecognised.

3.1 Miracle and Superstition

Whereas in the first years of the Christian community healing activities were associated with the local church and with individuals in the congregation who had this gift, later on we see such healing associated with particular leaders of the church, which in most cases led to their being considered to be saints. (It hardly needs saying that the term "saint" in the New Testament referred not to particularly holy people but to the members of the Christian community as a whole: the 'saved'.)

We are of course continually restricted by the paucity of the written evidence for the period so that the focus on the main characters may conceal something else going on in the background but nevertheless we become aware that over the centuries miracles of healing took place.

In time healings were attributed to the bones or relics of holy people. Justification for this was given on the basis of the woman being healed by touching Jesus' cloak, by the healing effect of Peter's shadow and of Elisha's bones. Elisha is cited by Origen,

Cyril of Jerusalem, Ambrose, Chrysostom, and other Church Fathers to justify this practice so it was clearly current long before the Middle Ages with which it is often associated.

(The following is taken from *The History of the Church* by Philip Schaff, Volume III: Nicene and Post-Nicene Christianity. A.D. 311-600.—Public Worship and Religious Customs and Ceremonies—Worship of Relics. Dogma of the Resurrection. Miracles of Relics)

The story is, that when Ambrose, in 386, wished to consecrate the basilica at Milan, he was led by a higher intimation in a vision to cause the ground before the doors of Sts. Felix and Nahor to be dug up, and there he found two corpses of uncommon size, the heads severed from the bodies (for they died by the sword), the bones perfectly preserved, together with a great quantity of fresh blood.

These were the saints in question. They were exposed for two days to the wondering multitude, and then borne in solemn procession to the basilica of Ambrose—performing on the way the healing of a blind man, Severus by name, a butcher by trade, and afterward sexton of this church. This, however, was not the only miracle which the bones performed. "The age of miracles returned," says Ambrose. "How many pieces of linen, how many portions of dress, were cast upon the holy relics and were recovered with the power of healing from that touch. It is a source of joy to all to touch but the extremist portion of the linen that covers them; and whoso touches is healed. We give thee thanks, O Lord Jesus, that thou hast stirred up the energies of the holy martyrs at this time, wherein thy church has need of stronger defence. Let all learn what combatants I seek, who are able to contend for us, but who do not assail us, who minister good to all, harm to none." In his homily De invention SS. Gervasii et Protasii, he vindicates the miracle of the healing of the blind man against the doubts of the Arians, and speaks of it as a universally acknowledged and undeniable fact: The healed man, Severus, is well known, and publicly testifies that he received his sight by the contact of the covering of the holy relics.

Jerome calls Vigilantius, for his opposition to the idolatrous veneration of ashes and bones, a wretched man, whose condition cannot be sufficiently pitied, a Samaritan and Jew, who considered the dead unclean; but he protects himself against the charge of superstition. We honour the relics of the martyrs, says he, that we may adore the God of the martyrs; we honour the servants, in order thereby to honour the Master, who has said: "He that receiveth you, receiveth me."

The saints are not dead; for the God of Abraham, Isaac, and Jacob is not a God of the dead, but of the living. Neither are they enclosed in Abraham's bosom as in a prison till the day of Judgment, but they follow the Lamb whithersoever he goeth.

Augustine believed in the above-mentioned miraculous discovery of the bodies of Gervasius and Protasius, and the healing of the blind man by contact with them, because he himself was then in Milan, in 386, at the time of his conversion, and was an eye-witness, not indeed of the discovery of the bones—for this he nowhere says—but of the miracles, and of the great stir among the people.

Despite the willingness of the Early Fathers referred to above to justify such practice it certainly seems to us to verge on the superstitious and to border on magic. Nevertheless it appears that healing did take place and that should be significant to the later discussion.

We are aware that one of the causes of the Reformation was the corruption in the church which centred on the selling of indulgences and holy relics. The situation had been aggravated when Crusaders returning from the Holy Land brought back many items which purported to be relics. Bits of bone and splinters of wood could be passed off as the body parts of a saint or fragments of the cross of Christ.

However alongside this corrupt practice, which nevertheless often convinced the gullible, there were still individuals who gave actual healing by their living ministry. One such was Bernard of Clairvaux.

Bernard is significant in this respect: not only are there accounts from third parties about his activities—which sceptics might relate to later attempts to promote his sainthood—Bernard himself refers to his own ability and marvels at it. Miracles, he said, had been wrought of old by saintly men and also by deceivers, but he was conscious neither of saintliness nor of fraud. He is reported as recognizing his own power, but as being reluctant to speak of it (*History of the Church, Volume V*). I find it interesting that he is reported as using various techniques. "Sometimes Bernard placed his hand upon the patient, sometimes made the sign of the cross, sometimes offered prayer, sometimes used the consecrated wafer or holy water."

Although, as today, there were one or two notable sceptics it certainly seems that Bernard of Clairvaux had a significant healing ministry. Certainly the age of miracles did not die with the Councils of the early Church.

Having said that, it is clear that the Roman Catholic Church took a particular path in dealing with miracles of healing. These have become associated with sainthood and are used as evidence to justify the canonisation of new saints. The last pope, John Paul II, has been somewhat precipitated into the canonisation process partly on the evidence of those who have been healed having prayed to him since his death. This seems to me to be a path which disconnects healing from the everyday, making it exceptional rather than an integral part of human life.

Nevertheless there have over the years continued to be

individuals who have had a special interest in healing. John Wesley had what many today would consider a quirky interest which, whilst encouraging the use of appropriate herbal and folk remedies, also led to his experimenting with an early form of electric shock therapy. At the same time there were accounts within the revival movement of what were categorised as miraculous healings not dissimilar from those described in the early centuries. In the twentieth century there were one or two leading thinkers who, whilst encouraging prayers for and an expectation of healing, also engaged with health professionals. In Methodism Leslie Weatherhead was particularly significant as was Morris Maddocks within the Anglican Church. Weatherhead encouraged congregational prayer and the use of techniques such as visualisation. Morris Maddocks as an Anglican was more sacramental in his approach. He also founded and led the Acorn Trust which has had a significant ministry in training within the field of healing and counselling.

The "disconnect" within the Catholic community was challenged in the mid-twentieth century by the growth of the Charismatic movement within the Church and specifically within the Roman Catholic Church's own congregations. It becomes more difficult to hold to the connection between "Saints" and healing when such things are happening within the worshipping community in full view of everyone.

It should be added that despite the attempts of Vatican II to distance the Church from the practice of the veneration of the saints, there remains, not surprisingly, within the folk practice of that church's members an enduring commitment to that form of spirituality and to the expectation of healing miracles associated with prayers to the saints. This is, for example, documented by Robert Orsi in *Between Heaven and Earth* in which he examines the practice of members of his own family who were immigrants to the United States from Italy. This may well have been reinforced by the personal convictions and emphasis of Pope John Paul II within whose time in office many more saints were canonised than had been the case for many previous pontificates.

3.2 Community Care

One place in which the integrated ministry of healing may well have continued was in the monastic movement, which by its very nature had more in common with the separated community of the early Church. Early Christians were marginalised by society, and perhaps by their own actions and priorities, but nevertheless continued to engage with the outside world. Those who chose to enter the monastic life formally separated themselves from the general society and formed themselves into self-sufficient communities. Under the pastoral leadership of their abbot the members of the community would produce and prepare their own food and would clearly care for one another's health needs.

According to the life of Bernard of Thiron, amongst the members of the Carthusian Order it was the custom in some convents for monks suffering from headache or other physical ailments to have the abbot place his hands on their bodies, trusting to his miraculous power for healing (Walter, *Die ersten Wanderprediger Frankreichs,* Leipzig, 1906, II. p. 50).

The Brothers of the Hospital of St Antonius were an order specifically dedicated to the care of the sick and poor. Their founder, Gaston, had prayed to St Anthony for his son who was suffering from the condition known as St Anthony's Fire. When his son survived they both committed themselves to a religious life. They had houses in France, Germany, Hungary and Rome and they were also credited with healing animals which led to a tradition of a procession of horses and cattle past their Rome Convent for a blessing each St Anthony's Day.

A major figure of the Middle Ages was Hildegard of Bingen whose influence is still felt today. As well as being a visionary and a musician, she also developed a system of healing using herbs and natural substances. She was particularly attached to the efficacy of Dinkel (spelt/ur-Wheat)—which as it happens is low in gluten—encouraging its use in various ways including as a filling for mattresses. Her story deserves to be studied. In his History of the Church, Schaff tells us that 'scarcely a sick woman came to her without being healed'. He continues, "Her power was exerted in the convent and outside of it and upon persons of both sexes. People from localities as distant as Sweden sought her healing power. Sometimes the medium used was a prayer, sometimes a simple word of command, sometimes water which, as in one case, healed paralysis of the tongue." (*History of the Church Volume V: The Middle Ages. A.D. 1049-1294.—The Monastic Orders—Monastic Prophets*)

So in Hildegard we see the two streams maintained—the pastoral and practical care of the sick together with the promotion of health, alongside a charismatic ministry of healing.

Whatever else was going on outside we also know that monasteries had herb gardens where plants with healing properties could be cultivated. So the knowledge of natural cures was preserved and developed.

Having introduced Hildegard of Bingen into this account I am reminded of Dorothee Sölle's book "Mystik und Widerstand" (Mysticism and Resistance) (Hoffmann und Campe Verlag, Hamburg 1997) in which Sölle suggests that institutional religion finds it hard to cope with individuals who do not conform, especially when that non-conformity is consequent upon a very direct sense of the divine. Thus I find it interesting that in the monasteries healing was the activity of the holy, whereas when practised in the outside community the same skills became associated, at least in the popular mind with witchcraft. Is this another example of the need for institutional control? This is by no means a frivolous question since we shall meet it in another way later on.

Those of us fortunate enough to have been brought up under a system of universal health care like the National Health Service in Britain can forget what it was like in earlier years. Those who could afford to pay did so but those who could not had to depend on charity. In most cases over the centuries that was provided by religious bodies. In Germany today there are still hospitals run and substantially staffed by members of religious orders, Protestant and Catholic. Even the numerically small United Methodist Church (EmK) has a general hospital in Wuppertal run as part of its Diakonie (diaconal) work. Catholic hospitals throughout the world with their nurses who are nuns are familiar to us all. And of course in the last centuries many medical missionaries were sent out to what we would now call developing countries taking the gospel message with them. The recent death of a doctor in Afghanistan working with a Christian programme to provide eye care is an indication that such work of healing continues today. (A Christian friend of ours worked for the same organisation in Kabul during the Russian occupation there. The staff members were expressly forbidden from public evangelism, so the main witness to their faith was through caring, and giving and receiving hospitality.)

The increasing scientific and medical understanding of the body and how it works has driven a fairly substantial wedge between the provision of care and the treatment of disease and injury. Recent cases of patient neglect in the UK lead many to question whether the medico-scientific competence has not led to the undermining of simple human compassion. This may well have been further undermined by the continuous attempts to reduce the costs of an expanding service.

It is notable that many hospices which are much more care-focussed than normal hospitals were founded by Christians or Christian charities. Their naming after Saints is another silent witness to the origins of that care.

3.3 Conclusion

The division between healing and caring was initially driven by an ignorance of human biology and anatomy. This inevitably led in some cases to superstition and the marginalisation of folk healers and generally to a theology of miraculous divine intervention to explain recovery from illness and disease. Caring for the weak and the dying was clearly a ministry for those who lived out the gospel command to "love your neighbour".

With the Enlightenment, the gradual acquisition of scientific knowledge, coupled with a less interventionist view of God reinforced the divide which has become very deep-seated today. One of our aims in trying to re-think our theology of healing should be to try to bridge this divide.

Chapter 4

What is healing?

In the Introduction and in the first chapter I referred to the difficulty of defining "healing" and mentioned Pilch's distinction between curing and healing. He related "cure" to "restoring a person to health or well-being" and healing to "restoration of meaning to life".

If we are honest about it, most of us think of healing in terms of expectation of cure. We hope to be restored to the health we have previously experienced. That is, frankly, why so many people are disappointed with the results of healing prayer.

Any thinking person will accept that physical deterioration is a characteristic of human life. No-one has any expectation of being able to reset the clock to when we were young fit and healthy—or in my case: young, not very fit and reasonably healthy. As we grow older we mature mentally and spiritually. When we are young we have more vitality but less knowledge of the world and less to reflect upon.

If I develop arthritis with my increasing years that is not surprising. In fact, given the genetic make-up of my family and the experience of the previous generation it will be unexpected if I do not experience arthritis. Similarly it will be surprising if the female members of my family do not succumb to cataracts of the eyes since they have been a common feature for several generations. Having three granddaughters I say that without any pleasure at all.

In the introduction I made reference to a man who came to healing services suffering from stomach cancer. He was already in the latter stages having previously been in remission. I am not sure what he expected—we never discussed it. It could be argued that the fact that he died showed he was not healed but in reality the strength and peace he received from healing prayers sustained him in the period leading up to his death. In fact he invited me, through his own priest, to visit him the evening before he died. And, as I wrote earlier, his wife continued for some time attending the weekly services. Dave was certainly not cured but I would maintain that he was healed insofar as his life and impending death found new meaning.

In the introduction I also referred to the effect that Stephen Pattison's *"Alive and Kicking"* had on me when, after long delay, I eventually got round to reading it. For years (20 or so) I had been engaged in a healing ministry which involved praying for healing for those who in some way or other were sick and had been irritated that so few other people in the church seemed to share what I had come to perceive as a priority of the Church's mission—which as a matter of fact I still do! However Pattison's point was that we seem to be asking God to intervene in the lives of individual people to "make them better" when they might have been better served if we had worked to prevent them becoming ill in the first place—not something that is normally on the agenda of the local church when considering mission.

Consider the following quotations from a BBC article in 2004:

'A woman born in Kensington and Chelsea has a life expectancy 6.8 years greater than one born in Manchester. In 1997-9, male life expectancy at birth was 71.1 years for unskilled manual men versus 78.5 years for professionals.'

And in the same article:

'The average consumption of fruit and vegetables among adults in England is less than three portions a day. Recommended amount is five

Less than two in five men do enough weekly physical

activity

Over one in five adults is obese. In 2001, 15% of 15 year olds were obese

A quarter of men and a sixth of women drink more than the recommended safe level' (of alcohol).

If we are concerned about health and wholeness then we need to address the causes of ill health as well as trying to help people who are already ill.

In *Why Zebras don't get Ulcers* Robert M Sapolsky discusses the causes of stress. This is, incidentally, a book well worth reading. One of his points is that if you wish to avoid stress then do not be born poor in a society of unequal wealth distribution. Being born poor in a uniformly poor society is not particularly stressful but living in the face of extreme wealth disparity is. The book rather puts the lid on the myth that stress is the domain of the professional classes.

If in Pilch's terms "healing is the restoration of meaning to life", and it seems to me to be a valid definition, then for many people in today's world the problem is not so much restoration as the actual introduction of the possibility of a truly meaningful life.

In the previous chapter I wrote about the bifurcation, the division, of healing and caring. There is a tendency in the modern church, I believe, to lose sight of the "social justice activities" of the Christian community as fulfilment of the Church's healing ministry. In fact I believe the Church has failed to affirm the importance of Jesus' second instruction to his disciples when he sent them out on mission (Luke 9:2). We have emphasised very much the importance of sharing the Good News through preaching but have underplayed the instruction to heal.

The irony is that regardless of formal objectives and perhaps without ever making the conscious connection, the Church has engaged in precisely those objectives of healing which I have suggested above relate to social care and combating injustice. As a Methodist my thoughts go immediately to Action for Children (formerly the National Children's Home) and Methodist Homes for the Aged (MHA) as well as Methodist Relief and Development Fund. These can of course be paralleled in other denominations and ecumenically e.g. The Children's Society, Christian Aid, Cafod. All these organisations and programmes are potentially engaged in aspects of healing even if it is not specifically named as an objective.

An example: For many years now MHA has sponsored the Live at Home Scheme in which elderly people are supported by volunteers and paid organisers to enable them to continue to remain in their own homes with a better quality of life. Insofar as the major pressure point on the health services in the coming decades is going to be how to deal with an increasing elderly population, anything which the Church and its agencies can do to delay the demand for medical and social care is obviously beneficial. For an individual, who for some reason or another has become isolated, to receive regular care from someone who is also able to access the other caring agencies or to act as an advocate is likely to mean that they can be dealt with before their needs are critical. I will refer to this in detail in a later chapter when I look at Parish Nursing.

However there is a danger in limiting ourselves to the institutional and thereby undermining the genuine effectiveness of what is traditionally considered to be "Healing Ministry". This was the reason that I delayed reading Stephen Pattison's "*Alive and Kicking*" when I was first offered it. It is absolutely clear to me that prayer, with or without the laying on of hands, still has a place in our Christian practice and that many still receive benefit from it but I really want to try to come to terms with the reality of that process.

4.1 How does healing work?

I want to raise some questions now and to suggest possible explanations before, in the next chapter, trying to construct a theological interpretation of what this implies.

Whenever the topic of healing is introduced in a local church setting where there has been no regular healing ministry there is almost always hesitation, or even resistance, because some people have been hurt, or at the very least disappointed, by previous experience of healing. Often this can be put down to inadequate preparation and inappropriate expectations. If people are expecting radical cures for chronic conditions they are generally likely to be disappointed. There are of course some healers who have seen such results, but even they would admit, I think, that these are relatively rare.

A more serious problem emerges when people are then told that the failure to recover is a result of either their unconfessed sins or their lack of faith. The possibility that failure results from a lack of faith on the part of the ones praying is also sometimes suggested, but spreading the blame in this way does not help in the least.

Related to that is the idea that someone has not been healed because God did not want them to be healed, that their suffering would serve a purpose. It is the same rationale as that used to explain the death of a child. I have to say that I personally find this totally unacceptable. I cannot believe in a loving God who intentionally inflicts pain because it will serve a useful purpose. I do however believe that pain and suffering can be redemptive and that we can learn both from our own experience and from the example of other people. So for me the idea that healing failed so that the person concerned could grow, or be a better witness, does not work at all.

Another ground for suspicion is the dubious experience of tele-evangelists and the like who, despite on the one hand appearing to have successful outcomes to prayer, have also been shown to be exploiting their ministry for personal gain and sometimes to follow an immoral lifestyle. It is a shame that this undermines what can otherwise be seen as a positive life-enhancing ministry.

For myself I have always tried to underplay the healing ministry and in particular avoided using it as a form of evangelistic bait to get people into the church. My understanding of the Gospels is that Jesus' priority was to preach and teach whilst his personal concern led to healing those who were in need. More than once he said it was time to move on because he needed to preach in another place—to share the good news. The healings were an objective outworking of the good news he was preaching. Naturally news travelled and people came to be healed but that was not Jesus' first priority.

In Berlin we gave only the smallest of space to details of the weekly healing service on the church notice board. Almost all who came did so on personal recommendation or invitation. Not surprisingly, however, a number of people who had not previously been church adherents began to worship in the congregation as a result of their experience of healing.

For those churches that have no regular ministry of healing it is also something that is seen as an exception rather than part of the normal ministry. That carries with it exceptional expectations. If you are going to make a special effort to do something then you tend to expect exceptional outcomes! If you have a continual ministry then weekly expectation will be less high, notwithstanding that sometimes significant healing takes place.

So can healing in the church only take place if a "specially gifted" person is present? Do we have to book someone to lead a mission? Or do we have to ordain someone specially to the function in the local congregation? In other words is the ministry of healing limited in time, person and setting?

Some interpretations of Paul's references to the Gifts of the Spirit lead us to think that they are given to individual people for the benefit of the Church. I indicated earlier in relation to Paul (page 31) that my understanding is rather that the gifts are given to the church and can be accessed when needed by whoever happens to be present and willing to take the risk of appearing foolish (fools for Christ?).

My experience on leaving one church of seeing the laying on of hands for healing stop because I was no longer there, though the prayer time did continue, led me to encourage much wider participation as we developed the work in Berlin. The experience seemed to confirm that if prayer with laying on of hands was necessary and none of the usual leaders were present the benefit could nevertheless be offered and received.

An example from Berlin: My colleague and I were away at a three day conference so one of the church members, who had been working with me on translating prayers for healing from English to German, said she would lead on the Wednesday evening. She admitted later that she had hoped no-one would attend! In the event my wife's father died that day in England and when she called to let me know I suggested she went to the healing prayers. The young lady who had hoped to sit alone in silence found herself ministering the laying-on of hands to someone in real pastoral need. Her ministry was on this occasion extremely effective. Lynda received a real sense of peace as Astrid laid hands upon her. She had received no special training, no ordination or authorisation except informally from me yet her willingness to act meant that an effective blessing was given.

I am sure that it is helpful to train people to have an effective healing ministry and also in the context of a local church community to give people due authorisation, but only as a matter of good order and not because healing will otherwise be blocked.

Having said all that, a major question remains. We have seen in an earlier chapter that throughout the history of the church there have been people with healing gifts, such as Bernard of

Clairvaux or Hildegard of Bingen. The question is whether this is God's power working through especially holy people or whether these people, being especially holy are attuned to mediate healing.

Returning to one of the problems above; if healing does not take place has God chosen not to act? Are we dealing with a God who gives or withholds healing according to a divine whim? As the reader might expect having reached this point, I really cannot accept such a view of God.

In discussion with a Baptist colleague over Parish Nursing we disagreed fundamentally as to whether Parish Nursing was a specifically Christian activity. She was of the opinion that healing could only be offered in the name of Jesus Christ and that it would therefore be impossible to do so as a member of the Hindu or Jewish community. Similarly I have read a book by a healing practitioner in Wales who expressed the view that if healing is offered other than in the name of Christ it is counterfeit and will in due course come to be seen as such.

I find both of these views totally unacceptable, mainly because there is ample evidence that true healing, especially in the wider definition which I have offered above, clearly takes place in other faith traditions and out of a similar response of care for the individual.

Many people with whom I have spoken refer to the basic core of the healing process as being a mutual bond between healer and healed expressed as: the healer wishes to offer healing and the other wishes to receive it. Put another way: the healer must love the one who is asking for healing and the recipient must love themselves. This seems to speak of open channels to one another.

So what in reality is going on? If only there were a simple answer! There do however seem to be some pointers and there are certainly developing studies in neurology and histology which give us an inkling, though since I am no authority in either field I can only speak from impression rather than detailed competence.

I wrote in the introduction of my colleague who, when I held my hand over his sore knee, deduced it must be microwaves. I have been doing this for long enough now to be sure that there seems to be some sort of energy transfer going on. (The number of times I have had an electric shock getting into a car makes me think naturally of static electricity!) I find that when I move my hand over the affected area I can often isolate what appears to me to be a "hot spot". I will then hold my hand over that location. A friend who had had quite severe back problems for a year asked me to move my hand over her back and to see what my impression was. I located a particular spot and indicated it to her. Later in the day she visited her physiotherapist and told her what I had found. The physiotherapist examined her and confirmed that I had located something and she gave her different treatment accordingly.

Logic tells me that if we have pain in our body it tends to show itself by inflammation, and inflammation, by its very name, implies heat. That could explain why sensitively exploring the body surface without touching it might enable the location of some problem. What it does not explain is why holding the hand over that point can then cause an alteration in the actual condition.

Consider this. My wife is lying face down, unable to see what I am doing. I move my hand above her body and each time I pass a particular spot she flinches. It is sufficiently painful that after a couple of times she asks me to stop. Clearly something objective was happening because she did not know where the hand was but at precisely the same point she experienced pain without any physical contact. In hindsight we might be able to deduce that what she had was inflammation in the abdomen caused by endometriosis coupled with a damaged gut as the result of wheat intolerance—but that is the result of decades of medical investigation and treatment! The point I am making here is that some sort of energy transfer was taking place which was independent of touch.

On one occasion when I was hospital chaplain, an elderly lady was experiencing pain from an infection in her leg on which she had a bandage. I held my hand over the spot (no physical contact) and shared the hope that the pain would dissipate. A little later passing the ward I popped in to see how she was. She was highly amused as well as relieved. Almost as soon as I had left her the inflammation had burst, absolutely soaking the bandages, and a nurse had had to change the dressing. She felt much more comfortable. It could of course have been a coincidence but I suggest it wasn't.

Now, what about intention on the part of the parties concerned? I have already said there needs to be openness to one another. I was leading a seminar as an "away day" for a church in Birmingham. I was talking about the way I lead prayers for healing and was demonstrating how and where I might place my hands. I reached out to the minister asking if I might use her as a guinea pig. She agreed. I was simply demonstrating a technique and certainly not consciously offering healing. Nor was she consciously expecting anything. Later on I was going into more detail and enlisted her services again. Before I could do anything she told the whole group that she had been having real problems with a frozen shoulder, sufficient to merit seeing a consultant. She then raised her arm to full height saying that when I had touched her shoulder earlier it seemed to have healed it. This was without prayer, without intent or expectation. It simply happened. I saw her again some months later and the problem had not recurred.

Apart from pain relief, on which I have to say I have a pretty good record, it is clear to me that often people with what might be termed mental or spiritual conditions benefit from receiving the laying on of hands. It could be that the exercise of sitting quietly and taking time to receive care is psychologically beneficial. It is of course none the worse if it is so.

There is in some circles a sort of unspoken assumption that if something can be categorised as psychological or psychosomatic it isn't a real problem. I was recently directed by a friend to the recording of a television programme on the ARD website in Germany regarding the interaction of mainstream medical services and alternative health practitioners. (The programme relates to a book by Joachim Faulstich *"Das Geheimnis der Heilung: Wie altes Wissen die Medizin verändert"*.) It was most interesting. Different therapies were used including the use of laying on hands to relieve pain. The example given showed the consultant on his rounds on an orthopaedic ward with the nursing staff. Whilst visiting one lady who had had a knee replacement the nurse gently moved her hands over the knee area. The patient said that it was very effective. From my own experience this is no surprise but I was delighted to see it being adopted in this context.

Elsewhere in the programme a specialist said that clearly prayer and meditation were helpful. Whether this indicated divine intervention or was a psychological effect resulting from the stimulation and relaxing of parts of the brain he could not say. The programme went on to show that the brain and the nervous system are capable of quite radical healing and presumably also the opposite. A central figure in the programme was a young Polish cellist who following a brain tumour had lost the function of a large part of his brain. Through visualisation and hypnotherapy he was enabled to relearn how to walk. He had not regained the use of his left arm. Later on the brain tumour began to grow again and he tried to resist the growth through visualisation. This did not appear to be working but his therapist suggested that instead of visualising the cancer and trying to destroy it he should visualise his good cells, of which of course there were far more, and concentrate on their overcoming the tumour. He told how he had gone for one of his regular brain scans with no great expectation and was thus not surprised when the specialist, with whom by now he had developed a fairly close relationship, returned in tears. He was however surprised to discover that they were tears of joy resulting from the information that the scan revealed that the tumour had completely disappeared.

I am no biologist and will leave it to others to put the right medical terms to what I am about to say. I understand that all the cells of the body are programmed to switch off and die when they have fulfilled their purpose and that sometimes the switch fails resulting in a cancerous growth. If that switch can be reactivated the cancer will simply die. If my understanding is correct it could explain why sometimes a tumour will suddenly go, following some form of healing therapy.

I am not unwise enough to suggest that we should be able to sort out all cancers by healing prayers. The death of my own brother from sarcoma leaves no room for starry eyes. It is nevertheless a tantalising thought. And certainly we have much to learn about the ability of the human mind to control and modify our body and metabolism.

Another example in the ARD programme was of a young Iranian woman whose wound after an operation simply refused to heal. She was referred to a doctor in general practice who also used the laying on of hands. He also gave her time to talk. She revealed that after a traumatic childhood experience in hospital she had a phobia about hospitals. She visited the doctor three or four times for laying on of hands. On the fourth time a couple of days later she had a powerful dream in the night and when she woke the wound was healing. The consultant who had referred her to the general doctor confirmed that the wound was now healing properly including the correct formation of scar tissue.

I have suggested earlier that there might be a transfer of energy in some way during laying on of hands. People often speak of experiencing a very hot feeling when the hands are held over them—even, I have to add, when my hands are physically quite cold.

This sort of process fits well with some other therapies like Raiki—though, as with one or two other alternative therapies, I have serious doubts about the explanations of what is happening as the theoretical basis of the practice.

What happens, though, to the energy transfer idea when we are enabling healing at a distance? When I was in Berlin I was approached by a church member on behalf of her aunt who lived in south west Germany, near Heilbronn if I remember rightly. She was suffering with depression and no treatment was having any effect. Would I pray for her?

I telephoned her and worked through all the alternative possibilities of psychiatric and psychological therapies discovering that she had tried most of them and, like the woman with haemorrhaging in the gospel story, had had little success. I told her to sit in her chair and imagine I was laying hands on her shoulders while I would picture myself doing so. We left it at that. Some few days later I asked the niece how her aunt was. She told me that the family said she was totally transformed. One could dismiss it as psychological self-deception or one could ponder whether there is a connection across distance which is not explicable by standard physics.

My wife Lynda had another strange experience when a congregation member requested healing for back pain. While we were both laying hands on the young woman Lynda had a strong intuition that she should ask her if one of her legs was shorter than the other. Having initially resisted asking such a strange question she eventually did so and it was indeed the case that one leg was shorter than the other. She was meant to wear an insole to compensate and also to attend a clinic for traction but did not like to do so because it used up too much of her "precious" time doing God's work. The healers' recommendation was to return to the doctor and follow the medical advice.

Having regularly attended the church for some months she never came again! Where did Lynda's intuition of this condition come from?

Incidentally, someone once brought a dog to our healing service and, not sure of the propriety of this, I laid hands on the dog before the service. He had had a stroke but within days he had recovered full mobility. Afterwards he used to come with his owners to the healing service and lie quietly through the proceedings. I share this but cannot begin to work through the implications!

Having said that it occurs to me that in the case of animals it is difficult to make the argument for a placebo effect whereas that is something which can be offered in the case of human beings who are aware of what may or may not be being offered. The commonest use of placebo is in medical trials to assess the effects and side effects of medications. The general expectation would be that taking a sugar pill would simply have no effect however when people are told that they are taking a stimulant many of them experience a higher pulse rate and raised blood pressure whilst their reaction time improves. The reactions work in the opposite direction when they are told they are taking a sleep-producing drug. Apparently this can happen even when the patient is actually told they are taking a placebo.

I am reminded of the famous "Hawthorn Experiments" which are familiar to anyone who has studied management. In these studies the investigators were attempting to show that performance in the factory would increase as working conditions improved. The initial results backed up this hypothesis completely. However when the experimenters started worsening the working conditions the performance still improved. The conclusion was that the workers performed better because they were the subject of an experiment and they felt valued. One can see how similar effects might be derived in the context of health and healing. It is certainly one reason for arguing that patients need time with their doctor or other therapist so that they feel valued.

In both of these examples it is clear that when we are engaging with people as individuals we are dealing with a complex interaction of body, mind and spirit. Any system of health care which ignores this fact is always going to be deficient. For this reason we should beware of simply dismissing healings associated with what we might consider to be superstition as also the reality of sickness which is caused by beliefs in magic and cursing.

I have recently read *My Stroke of Insight* by Jill Bolte Taylor a brain scientist who suffered a major stroke as the result of a brain haemorrhage. She describes how it felt when only the right side of her brain was working. She said that without the controlling and limiting functions of the left side brain which define time and distance she found herself at one with the universe. She imagines it is the state that Buddhists would describe as nirvana. It could of course be psychological nonsense or it could be an indication that at some level we are capable of relating to others who are also part of this whole universe.

For me this idea fits in as well with the idea of being "one in Christ" and of being "the Body of Christ in the world". But perhaps I am trespassing on the next chapter.

4.2 Conclusion

My experience tells me that there are aspects of healing which are not adequately explained at present by medicine or physics but which are near enough to the boundaries of these disciplines to be considered more acceptable than the idea that prayer will somehow catch the attention of God who will then decide whether or not to respond on the basis of the individual's merits and circumstances. There is a long way to go but we should at least allow ourselves to be open-minded.

Chapter 5

A Theological Reflection

I have attempted in the preceding pages to indicate my own practical experience over the past number of years and also the way in which healing seems to be present in the world as we all experience it. It is hardly surprising if this challenges some traditional Christian understanding of what is involved in the process of healing, especially when seen from the perspective of spiritual healing in response to the commission of Christ.

Before I take this further I need to make another personal statement so that the reader does not spend fruitless time trying to second guess where I am heading. I do this because I have read the work of one or two contemporary theologians recently and have had my doubts about what they actually believed. I found this distracting.

I want also to say that I feel that each one of us, if we reflect with integrity on our own circumstances at any particular point in our lives, will come to an understanding of God which reflects that point and the knowledge and experience we have had to date. As we get older, our life experience will bring us new insights and knowledge which we could not have had at an earlier stage. These do not, however, negate those earlier beliefs which were held with complete integrity. If that is true of my personal journey then it follows that I have to affirm other people who are currently at a different point in their own voyage of spiritual discovery from the one I have reached, even if I disagree with them. I say this because I do not expect everyone to agree with me. But I do ask that what follows is read with a mind open to possible new insights and with an appreciation that what I suggest is offered with genuine integrity.

My personal faith is rooted in the Resurrection of Jesus. I have no doubt at all that Jesus was crucified and that he was experienced as a living presence subsequent to his publicly attested death. I cannot conceive of how the dispirited group of leaderless disciples could possibly have been transformed into evangelists who were willing to risk and even lose their lives as a result of sharing their conviction that this Jesus was still alive. Whether or not it was 'the Resurrection of the body' in a physical sense I do not know. A very strange physical body it must have been if it could appear and disappear and was sometimes not recognisable. What is absolutely clear to me is that Jesus was still alive after his physical death and that therefore there is an existence which is of a different order from the one we experience through our physical senses.

Secondly, I have always been distinctly uncomfortable with atonement theology, especially which which relates to blood sacrifice and the demands of divine justice. I am struck by the fact that in the gospels Jesus sends out the disciples to preach the good news that the Kingdom of God is present. Although Jesus speaks of his forthcoming death at various points in the accounts it seems clear to me that the message he was offering was not contingent upon that death. That his death was an almost inevitable consequence of his presentation of the good news, which was a challenge to the religious establishment in particular but also in that time probably inflammatory to the delicate political balance, is almost self-evident and I think this gospel message always will be.

As I read the gospel accounts, Jesus addressed most especially those who were excluded by society, particularly religious society, as being unworthy of God's acceptance. Jesus by his own actions in reaching out to the literally or figuratively untouchable (lepers, prostitutes, tax collectors) and also through his teaching (The Good Samaritan, The Prodigal Son) presented a God who was not looking for religious ritual purity or, come to that, religious orthodoxy, but rather a God who loved the creation and creatures unconditionally and wished them to respond accordingly. In a time when the majority of people believed in God or gods it was not a matter of convincing them that God existed; rather it was the assurance that they could live their lives under God's grace, expressing their love and gratitude by the way they lived in relation to one another.

Clearly the reality of the Resurrection events influenced the way the apostles interpreted what Jesus' life and teaching meant but it seems to me that each interpretation drew on the context of the people in their own time and with their own religious framework. Clearly if your own religious thinking has been formed by and centred in the Temple Cult with its sacrificial system it is inevitable that any explanation of the crucified Messiah will draw on that sacrificial imagery. If you are coming into contact with Christianity from a Gentile context it might well include sacrificial imagery but it will be of a different order since the relationship of Gentiles and their gods was different from that of the Jews with Yahweh.

Paul came to faith in Christ as a result of a striking personal experience on the Damascus Road, but that personal experience and his subsequent teaching could hardly fail to be influenced by his own upbringing and training as a Pharisee.

Anyone reading this will by now be clear that I am in no way a biblical literalist. I believe that the Bible contains the truths we need to be truly whole, or saved but that this comes from understanding the whole context and content rather than laying too much weight on individual verses and texts. It is from this standpoint that I now seek to explain what I want to call a "theology of healing".

I think I should also make clear that I have never considered myself an "academic" theologian—by which I mean that I have not read systematically the works of the great theologians with a view to synthesising, so to speak, a satisfactory theology for myself. In truth, in attempting to sort out my own thoughts to write what follows, I have read more theology than for most of my years in ministry. What I find enormously encouraging is that other more competent theologians have come to similar conclusions to some of those which I draw here.

5.1 Healing as part of the created order.

As I have suggested earlier, many of the problems associated with healing relate to the concept of an intervention by God to overrule what appears to be the natural order. I also wrote earlier about medical anthropology which seeks to enable understanding of medical conditions and healing through the eyes of the particular society in which it takes place (or does not as the case may be). Twenty years or so ago it was common for people to spend weeks in hospital following joint replacements. The speed with which most people today are back in action might be described as miraculous. It is certainly amazing! It does not mean however that God is popping into the operating theatres and giving the surgeons supernatural powers.

Similarly when my mother developed cataracts in her early 60s it was just before the general availability of lens implants and the surgeon was not prepared to risk doing one in view of the uncertainty of how long it would last. She therefore had to suffer the inconvenience of wearing contact lenses for nearly 25 years having spent months after each of the two operations avoiding tipping her head forward. Many reading this will know of people who today go into the hospital outpatients in the morning returning home with an eye patch and being able to see almost immediately—a "miracle" of science and medical skill. If all surgeons were convinced Christians we might speak of their skill being God-given and in fulfilment of their Christian ministry. But what of those who are equally skilled, caring and successful who are of another faith or probably none? Does God intervene surreptitiously on behalf of patients who are the subject of prayer from the believing community without the surgeon knowing, so that he or she is guided like a puppet? That seems to me hard to imagine (especially when plenty of people are successfully operated upon without such faith community support).

I have written earlier of my belief that healing power is not restricted to those who, within the faith community, are specially trained and commissioned. I think I would want to go further than this and suggest that such healing power is within every living person if only we would seek to find it and then have the confidence to use it.

At the simplest level consider what happens when a child hurts him- or herself? An adult, usually the parent, will take the child, perhaps give it a hug or rub the spot that has been hurt, giving comfort. Is that all that it is? Or by that action are we actually administering healing, perhaps actually giving healing energy? I ask the question without knowing the answer but if the use of the hands in healing ministry has a genuine effect why should it not be so in this form of comforting? If being still and quiet helps adults to recover their mental balance why shouldn't it be so for children?

Then what about the way the human body works? When you stop to think about it, it is indeed almost miraculous! To quote Jill Bolte Taylor in *My Stroke of Insight* (p14)"the typical adult human body is composed of approximately fifty trillion cells. That would be 8,333 times all of the six billion people on the planet! What's amazing is that this huge conglomeration of bone cells, muscle cells, connective tissue cells, sensory cells, etc. tend to get along together to generate perfect health". If you cut yourself the body will heal the cut. If you break a bone it will mend, although it might need help to return to its normal shape. (I have a friend whose fingers are somewhat misshapen as the result of playing cricket and rather too regularly breaking one or another when batting or keeping wicket!)

On balance it is hardly surprising that sometimes the process does not quite work properly or gets out of hand—after all, fifty trillion cells!!

The implication of this is that healing is built into the natural order. It is, if you like, God-given. From what I have said above it will be clear that I do not take the Genesis account of creation literally, but I can accept the idea that Creation is God-inspired and also that there is a purpose and a direction within it. God declared it "good".

When I was studying theology in preparation for ministry I was interested in the idea of the Holy Spirit in Creation. Specifically, I was interested in the way that God seems to be close when we are in surroundings of natural beauty—the majesty of the mountains, the vastness of the dark night sky, the intricate uniqueness of a snowflake. In that context I read something by the eminent theologian Wolfhard Pannenberg who suggested that the Holy Spirit was present in the evolutionary process through the mechanism of self-transcendence; that all organisms have a tendency to complexity rather than simplicity which means they transcend their current state and become something "higher". This, admittedly anthropocentric, model sees the human being as towards the top of this hierarchy of self-transcendence suggesting that we human beings have reached the point of recognising the possibility of awareness of a spiritual realm. I hope I have not done Pannenberg a disservice by this description—I read him nearly 30 years ago in the library and cannot therefore refer back to it! (I have recently had a chance to look at his later work and see he developed his thinking beyond this point.) Be that as it may, I personally find it a helpful model. It gives a direction to creation and also to human life. Included within the model is the possibility of wholeness—becoming what we are intended to be.

5.2 Is healing in the Church any different?

If you follow the argument of the previous section you are likely to ask whether there is relationship between this view of healing as an integral aspect of the natural order and the process we would consider is underway during prayers for healing within or outside of the liturgical setting of the church.

If people attend one of my regular healing services what are they going to experience; in what way will God be active in any healing which they receive? Clearly, for me at least, if we meet together in a church framework then we are doing so with an expectation of "drawing close to God" or of focussing upon God's presence in our lives. We are already oriented towards a sense of God's presence. That may not necessarily be true for someone attending for the first time as a "guest" but even they will attend with some sort of expectation. To that extent the Spirit of God will be more active than if it were a secular and/or medical setting. By that I do not wish to imply that God is not present in a medical centre, simply that where there is an expectation, God is more likely to be sensed.

If that is the case, is the Holy Spirit (God?) especially present in the prayerful laying on of hands? Again I would suggest that the setting enables a greater receptivity on the part of the person receiving prayer than might otherwise be so and might also aid the one ministering the healing. I referred earlier to the fact that for some the offering of healing in the context of Holy Communion/Eucharist is a significant act. I come from a much less sacramental background and am therefore far less attached to that liturgical context, though it has not prevented me from using it if circumstances permit or dictate.

If all of life is potentially sacramental, which I do believe, then there is no time or place where healing cannot be offered or received, and God, who is present in all times and in all places, can sanctify the moment by being present and active. I have coined the phrase "prayer by body language" to explain how an informal healing touch can be just as effective as a formal, or for that matter informal, prayer in a liturgical or pastoral setting.

An anecdotal aside: My wife met a congregational member in a local store. Conversation led to my wife placing her hand on the other person's back which was hurting. The lady concerned experienced strong warmth and the pain was relieved. She also experienced a sense of liberation that healing could be offered so simply.

We are speaking here of something more than simple caring touch and we are also talking about something different from routine medical care. But I would contend that it is no more miraculous, nor does it denote any greater intervention from God than do the less exceptional forms of caring, be it in the home or the hospital.

I am sure though that when we focus on being at one with God we are likely to be more able to access that power which seeks to draw all things into wholeness.

5.3 What of the Holy Trinity?

This may appear a strange question but it arises from the response of a colleague when I was sharing my sense that healing was more "creation theology" (not **creationist** I emphasise) than charismatic. That is it is part of the natural order of the world and life rather than an unnatural intervention. He said: "You are talking of the Logos as the agent of healing then." This was what the Germans call an "Aha-Erlebnis" (literally an "Aha!" experience) — a lot of things suddenly fell into place, the penny dropped!

For a number of years now I have felt drawn to the value of identifying Jesus with the Logos, as of course John does in the prologue to his Gospel. Without having read about Plato and the Stoic philosophers I still felt it was significant that the word "Logos" or "Word" was used to relate to Christ. There is no value in "Word" unless there is communication. The very use of the term *Word* has to imply a God whose nature includes a need, a desire, and a purpose to communicate. And for me this desire to communicate was given full expression in Jesus. Since this became apparent to me it has also always seemed that when Jesus spoke it was the Word of God, the Reason of God that was communicating not simply the man Jesus. Thus when Jesus says, "I am the Way the Truth and the Life. No-one comes to the Father except by me," it can be understood as the words of the Logos, that is God's communicating nature, rather than the words of Jesus, the time– and culturally-conditioned Galilean. I first used this interpretation in the context of a disagreement over inter-faith celebrations in school, but that is another story which I will come to in due course (Chapter 6). I know that I am not alone in this interpretation though I suspect scholars who claim that it was not John's intention may be correct. I have however heard it argued by Professors James Dunn and Frances Young, for both of whom I have great respect (see below, page 76).

In John's prologue all things were made through the Word. In Genesis the Spirit of God hovered over the deep. In the Wisdom of Sirach, in the Apocrypha, it was the Wisdom of God who was the agent in Creation. These are different ways of expressing the purpose of God unfolding through the divine action of creation. Clearly the use of separate nouns to describe the subject and object of the creative act makes us think in terms of separate beings. Is there a distinction between the person typing this paragraph and the one thinking about what to say?

I had better come clean here! I have a real problem with what might be described as the traditional understanding of the Trinity. On one hand it seems that some of the accepted conciliar definitions are far too anthropomorphic, albeit whilst at the same time trying desperately not to be. Much sacred art in its depiction of the Trinity uses the images of an old man, a young man and a dove. Granted there are variations, but you get the drift. I have read of the concept of a dynamic relationship within the Trinity, but actually that doesn't make much sense to me either.

Clearly the doctrine of the Trinity comes out of the experience of the church and is in other words an attempt to develop a theology which reflects that experience. I am of course trying to do the same in this book so let me state my case.

I prefer the following (and you can attach whatever heretical label best fits!): God's eternal nature includes a desire to communicate with the world/universe God has made. The Old Testament shows through the experience of the Israelites how difficult it is for people to appreciate the Divine, despite prophets and providential guidance. People need people if they are to see what love is in practice and they need teachers to explain what that means. Jesus was God's way of communicating with us. In Jesus God's nature was as fully expressed as it could possibly be within the limits of time, space and a human life. After Jesus' death and resurrection the disciples experienced his continuing presence with them and recognised the inspiration they received, in interpreting and preaching the scriptures, as being consistent with what he taught them during his lifetime. That spiritual presence is sometimes called the Spirit of God and sometimes the Spirit of Christ. All three—Jesus the man, the Spirit of God and the Spirit of Christ—are all the same thing: God in communication; but not in internal introspective communication; in communication with the Creation—with us.

In Rowan Williams' book "*On Christian Theology*" he manages a superb sweep through the relationship between the Spirit and the Word from the patristic period to the present day. In the end he seems to have found a satisfactory formula to differentiate between them but I am afraid I still find it somewhat contrived. I think, if I understand it rightly, he was seeking to define the Word as the communicating principle and the Spirit as the agent which draws us to God. I hesitate to disagree with so eminent a theologian as the Archbishop of Canterbury but I really can't see any difference. It seems to me really to be assigning a function of the Word as the one who reveals God's nature to a different agent so that the Trinity can be maintained. But then, I am not really very hot on the importance of maintaining tradition for its own sake!

Anyway, in the context of healing we ought not to differentiate between the work of the Spirit and the work of the Creator—be that God the Father, the Spirit or the Word. If it is acceptable that healing is part of the creative process then we cannot expect the process to be "short-circuited" by supernatural intervention. Where such things appear to take place—and they certainly do happen on occasion—it is not because the laws of the natural order have been broken or overruled. Rather it is that something has happened which we do not as yet understand.

I suspect some will ask where this leaves Jesus in the context of the Trinity. For me the idea that the human Jesus was eternally present with the Father does not make any sense. I am uneasy with the image of his being "sent down" from heaven to live amongst us. It smacks a little of space fiction and Doctor Who. The converse, that God's Word/Spirit, which by definition always existed, was present in the human Jesus and that he was thus indeed the incarnation of the living God, I can feel comfortable with. I simply resist any imagery which implies a two-tier universe, or pictures heaven as a glorified royal court, which was of course an appropriate metaphor for the 1st Century and beyond during which time the Throne of the Emperor was the pinnacle of an extremely powerful political structure.

Thus for me, if in evangelical terminology I "invite Jesus into my life" it is no different from inviting God into my life or, for that matter making myself open to the power of God's Spirit. In any event personally I do not really think we should pray to Jesus. We can come to God in Jesus' name—with his authority because we live in obedience to his teaching and example—but to approach Jesus seems to me to be a lesser course. I am happy to concede however that for those who find the human personal image helpful it almost certainly makes devotional sense.

In the course of preparing this material I have been reading Alan E Lewis's *"Between Cross and Resurrection — A Theology for Holy Saturday"*. This book provides an analysis of the history of Trinitarian theology but particularly a reflection on the devastation of the absence of God in the day between Good Friday and Easter Sunday. When it comes to the conclusions he draws for the application of the Gospel in the modern world I found myself agreeing with most of them, but I did so notwithstanding the premises on which he had based them.

His thesis, as I understand it, is that Easter Saturday reveals a God who eschews power, entering into the powerlessness of the grave. The only true power is love. For me he goes a step too far in "placing" God in the grave with/in Jesus which he describes as a transformative event for the future history of human life and the world.

I have no doubt that God is in the processes which I would describe as healing, but I do not see the events of Good Friday and Easter Saturday as being objectively transformative, objectively altering the world.

However I am sure that the power of the imagery of the cross, which reveals the consequences for Jesus of his total obedience to the priorities of God, can and does have transformative effects. And similarly I happily accept that Jesus' total identity with God means that God was present in the horror of the crucifixion.

This does rather emphasise, I think, that God is not an external impersonal force, but is one into whom, and into whose purposes we can enter. The aspect of God which draws us into this relationship can be variously described as the Word, the Spirit or the Lord Jesus. Which one draws us personally depends more on ourselves and our faith journey than on the interior nature of God.

5.4 Does healing have to be in the name of Jesus?

From a personal point of view I would maintain that as a committed Christian whose life is centred in Christ, on any occasion when I offer healing, whether by prayer or by touch, I am doing so as part of the body of Christ and implicitly in the name of Jesus, even if I do not necessarily use those particular words. And as I suggested above I find it difficult to distinguish between praying to God and coming to God in the name of Jesus.

What is more contentious though is the matter of whether healing can be offered other than in the name of Jesus. There is an ambiguity in the New Testament about people acting in the name of Christ though not part of the inner circle. It is sometimes rejected and sometimes affirmed. I suspect it has to do with motivation and that this should probably inform our judgement today.

The idea of acting in someone's name is based on acting with that person's authority and therefore in the way that they themselves would act. Jesus claimed he was acting in the name of his Father who had sent him and that anyone who acted in his name would be doing the will of his Father. If that be the case then it ought to be possible to act in accordance with the will of the Father without necessarily referring to the Son. This is where for me the concept of the Logos comes into play. As far as I can see, the Logos, as the communicating principle of God (in Christian terms "the Father") is not limited to the person of Jesus. Any extent to which God communicates and is sensed to be present is a consequence of the function of the Logos. This means that God can be experienced beyond the confines of the Christian faith. "No-one comes to the Father" except through the communicating power of the Word, which was most fully but not only expressed in Christ.

If all healing is an expression of the reconciling and saving nature of God, who is seeking to bring to completion that which is at present provisional, then whoever seeks to offer healing is conforming to the purposes of God and is acting in accordance with the divine will as mediated by the Logos.

5.5 Going with the flow.

A recent radio programme described the essential characteristic of the Chinese philosophical and religious tradition of Daoism as "going with the flow". I think it meant that we should stop striving to make our own way but should find the way which we are intended to take. Otherwise and scripturally expressed: "Be still and know that I am God", or as the Revised English Bible has it: "Let be then; learn that I am God". There is a distinction between disengaged quietism and "letting be". I like the analogy of white water canoeing which suggests that once you are within the right flow you can travel with speed although it can be extremely hard work staying within the flow. It is no easy way forward. It may sometimes be exhilarating but there is always danger lurking around the corner threatening to distract or even destroy you.

In *Between Cross and Resurrection* Alan E Lewis wrote of the problem of the immutability of God in relationship to the Cross. Reflecting on Barth and Jüngel he says this (page 189): "Far from static and immobile, God's way of being eternal involves forward movement characteristic of temporal existence, though in God's time the past is not lost nor the future unreachable. Hence Jüngel's summation of Barth's ontology: 'God's being is in becoming'. Becoming is not what identifies the creature over against the Creator... but a living, kinetic, active existence which is God's way of being God." In the sense of the illustration above being "still" could be interpreted as entering into a God in stasis whereas "letting be" is willingly cooperating with a God "in becoming".

If we can accept the idea that there is a divine purpose in Creation and that we are part of a process which leads ultimately to the whole Creation being brought to its perfect state of completion (salvation/health/wholeness) then ultimately our sole purpose in life should be to discern that process and to become one with it – to share in God's "becoming".

It seems to me that anything which could be described as "integrative" is godly whilst anything which tends towards disintegration is ungodly. That can be translated in health and wholeness terms as: anything that promotes and maintains health and wholeness of body, mind and spirit is a godly activity and to the extent to which we engage in it we are engaging in Kingdom activities and are inspired, empowered, by God's Spirit to do so. To be able to assent to dogmatic principles is unnecessary. "By their fruits you will know them".

This clearly makes nonsense of any assertion that just because the name of Jesus has not been attached to an act of healing it must be counterfeit. In fact the reverse can apply—as happened in the New Testament—if the name of Jesus is attached but without the integrity of intent and action on behalf of the person ministering it will be an ungodly action and should be condemned.

5.6 What about prayer?

If we have a problem with an interventionist God in the context of healing it is reasonable to ask how we can deal with prayer. When I made my serious commitment to God in 1975 or thereabouts (I can tell you the precise place but not the date!), I put myself entirely into God's hands asking that God direct my actions and my words. From that point on, prayers for myself have been difficult since the very act of asking seems like a betrayal of trust. Better that I try to find myself in the centre of God's will and purpose; that often requires stillness and silence rather than words. But that is personal to me.

However, what I feel relative to myself is not much removed from what I consider prayer for others should be. I really do not believe that we can change events by asking God to intervene.

And I do not think that we can ask God to go against the natural order (broadly interpreted as above) to effect some special healing. What I do believe, however, is that if we are at one with God's purposes and if we make ourselves available as instruments of healing, things will happen which otherwise might not have taken place.

As I mentioned earlier, at an ecumenical meeting in the West Midlands a United Reformed Church colleague uttered the following initially shocking remark: "We don't have prayers of intercession in our church anymore". He then added: "We only have prayers for healing." I like that. In the final analysis all prayers of intercession or petition are indeed seeking healing.

Sometimes people come to a healing service with a concern for someone else. I often suggest that they focus on the individual concerned, whom I usually do not know, while I focus on them. Obviously what I am trying to do is to direct some kind of healing to the third person via the one who has a loving relationship, thus accessing that bond of love.

Ultimately this is about trying to move within the flow of creative love.

5.7 Can places be healed?

I recall reading a pamphlet in Germany which included details of a service of blessing for the new airport at Munich. At the time I was mystified as to what the people concerned thought they were doing. I can understand providing prayer rooms and chapels at airports and presumably dedicating them for use, but what is the objective result of blessing an airport going to be? Fewer accidents? Better staff relations? A pleasant atmosphere to calm frustrated travellers? No. I still don't understand it.

However, I cannot deny that there are some places which make people feel uncomfortable and other places that seem to be blessed or sacred. Curiously, you might think, for a Christian, one of the most prayerful places I have ever visited was the Al-Aqsa

Mosque in Jerusalem. A friend visiting us in Lichfield went out for a walk and returned asking what the significance was of the church down the road. It had felt amazingly holy. It was St Chad's Church which is built on the site of the hermitage of St Chad himself who lived there in the 7th Century. Strangely my wife had had a similar experience there.

You might be able to think of places which have the opposite effect, which, so to speak, give off "bad vibes". Most of us have had the experience of sensing a bad atmosphere between people, but of course there is body language to betray it. A friend visiting the concentration camp at Sachsenhausen would not approach the former crematorium because the sense of what had happened there was too real. Sometimes things can be put down to excessive imagination but at other times there is no sensible explanation.

I mentioned earlier the reaction of the daughter who came into her mother's house after we had prayed for healing and asked what had happened because 'The house feels different'.

Many ministers find themselves being asked to pray for houses because the people living there think there is a malign presence. I was told of an old people's home where the residents kept hearing monks chanting. It transpired that the home had been built on the site of a monastery. A local minister was asked to help and he conducted prayers in the house. Whether anything objective happened is difficult to judge but the residents stopped complaining.

I was once asked to visit a house which the family claimed was being attacked by a poltergeist and in which there was supposedly the ghost of a baby. I went and talked with the family and having prayed with them I went and prayed in the places which seemed to be causing the disturbance. I didn't sense any presence, malign or otherwise, but left them anticipating that the pastoral support might do some good. A few days later the local newspaper reported that the home had been exorcised by "the local Methodist vicar"! The visit and the prayer had apparently been successful.

I cannot help wondering whether people and events leave some sort of imprint on places – whether physical things can have a memory. I have heard it suggested that a reason for homeopathy working, when scientifically there is nothing but water in the mixture because the dilution is to a sub-molecular level, could be that the water actually retains a memory of what it had previously been. That sounds like absolute nonsense in terms of the laws of physics, but sometimes it is necessary to ask whether these laws actually are the only set of criteria which work in our created environment.

I am aware that I asked a question at the beginning of this section that I have not really answered but it does remain as a question which needs to be considered.

5.8 Conclusion

My experience—and I do not think I am in any way unique in this—is that at various points in my life I have sensed that I was "in the right place". I can recall a morning in Berlin some weeks after we had arrived there, when, travelling on the local bus, I had a very strong sense of being where I was meant to be. In the terms of section 5.5 above, I sensed that I was going with the flow. Other things happened in the weeks and months following which continued to confirm this.

Similarly there have been occasions when, in the context of healing, one has felt oneself to be precisely in the place where one was meant to be. I used to find that when I was ministering healing in a bilingual setting I was concentrating more on trying to find an acceptable and grammatically correct German phrase to use as a closing prayer than I was on the person and their perceived needs. Nevertheless their response was often amazement that the words spoken were "spot on" for what they needed. It seemed, and seems to me, that this is an example of simply being immersed in the flow of the healing and loving grace of God. Undoubtedly the people who met, and especially those who were healed by, Jesus will have sensed that divine presence.

Today, those who are introduced to a new sense of health and wholeness, even if that means being reconciled to terminal illness, are also experiencing the working of God, Logos, Spirit through the ministry of those who seek to bring this about, whether they are Christians or not.

This does not in any way undermine or diminish the Christian gospel or the role of the Christian community in witnessing through word and action to the example given in the life death and resurrection of Jesus Christ but it should at the very least prevent us from the sin of arrogance which allows the suggestion that God can only work through us and those of our kind.

Chapter 6

Healing the World

In considering the nature of healing in Chapter 4 I suggested that authentic healing is going to function at the level of health promotion and social justice as well as on a one to one level of personal care and within a liturgical setting. If that is the case then we can use a healing model, focussed in the Word of God to deal with our engagement in the world. I would like to propose a model of Church as therapeutic community and in the last chapter I will suggest how that can appear in practical terms. However I referred earlier to the "Aha-*erlebnis*", penny dropping moment, when a colleague suggested healing as an activity of the Logos and I would like to explain why it was so important.

6.1 Healing the "clash of cultures"—Inter-faith dialogue.

I referred above (page 63) to using the "I am the Way, the Truth, the Life" quotation from John 14:6 in the context of a disagreement over inter-faith celebrations in a school. A grandparent had written proudly in a church magazine of the courage of her granddaughter in refusing to take part in Divali celebrations at her school even though the teacher had allowed her to do the narrative rather than to be an actor. I wrote in response that I regretted this and in doing so suggested that if we interpret John 14:6 as referring to the Word of God rather than limiting it to the man Jesus we have a far more open field for perceiving God in communication and we will inevitably be more tolerant of other faiths. I was not at the time aware of anyone else taking this particular line

Some years later, in preparation for going to work abroad in 1994, Lynda and I attended an inter-faith conference at

Swanwick. One of the speakers, Inderjit Bhogal, used the same text and argument in the context of inter-faith dialogue. This I found quite encouraging. At a follow-up conference on "The Uniqueness of Christ in the Context of Inter-Faith Dialogue" exactly the same case was made by Professor James Dunn in his presentation. As we met shortly afterwards in a small group I asked him if there was a body of writing on this topic. His response was that he did not think so but it seemed to him self-evident!

In April 2003 during a 'Building Bridges' seminar held at Doha, Qatar, Professor Frances Young made exactly the same point in her presentation *Christian Scripture and the Other* (see *Scriptures in Dialogue* ed. Michael Ipgrave, p109). With reference to John 14:6 she says 'The fundamental perspective (is that) the Word is with God, and indeed is God—for it is through him that everything was made. Nothing has come into being without him. Life is in him, and life and light is for humankind. Of course this 'Wisdom-like' Word is the way, the truth and the life, for all human creatures; and because of his relationship both with all created things and with God, how else could anyone have access to the Father?'

As with James Dunn I was able to discuss this with Frances Young in person at a study day and confirm that her interpretation is substantially similar to the conclusion I had reached.

By now, presumably, it will be obvious why I was so taken with the suggestion of the Logos as the agent of healing. For years I had intended to try to write something about the Logos in the context of inter-faith dialogue and here was another topic linking with the same context. Now at the most obvious level one might respond that if the Logos is "in relationship ... with all created things and with God" then any given topic will have a Logos perspective and that is probably correct. However the idea of God's reason, which enables all things to move towards the perfection for which they were intended, being directed into not only healing of individual relationships—which is not uncommon in the context of healing ministry—but also the healing of the greatest rifts between cultures and belief systems, adds an extra dimension to what we normally consider to be the subject matter of healing.

Notwithstanding what I wrote earlier, I believe the first impetus to think about inter-faith dialogue and the uniqueness of the Christian Gospel came during my study time in Manchester when we had two sets of neighbours, both from immigrant communities. On one side was a family who attended a local Pentecostal church; on the other was a family of former Ugandan Asians who were of the Hindu faith. The "Christian" family were typical of the infamous "family from Hell"—the husband abused his wife; the teenage boys were delinquent; the slightly younger girl was always in trouble at school. In contrast the members of the "Hindu" family were delightful neighbours—they fed the cat and watered the plants when we were away; they were always friendly and they invited us to their daughter's wedding (having invited Lynda to the loose equivalent of the 'hen party'). I emphasise that this is in no way intended as an exercise in stereotyping as it might have worked the other way round in another neighbourhood. However I could not help reflecting that the ones who exhibited the "fruits of the Spirit" were not the practising Christians but those of another faith.

In Matthew 7:15-20, Jesus—speaking of false prophets—says, "you will know them by their fruits", a good tree can't bear bad fruit nor a bad tree good fruit. In Galatians Paul lists the fruits of the Spirit (Galatians 5:22-23) as indicative that one is in Christ. I suppose that over the years I have come increasingly to believe that it is in our behaviour that we show our relationship to God and certainly not in our affirmation of dogmatic statements of faith.

Jesus also summarised the Law: "Hear, O Israel; The Lord our

God, the Lord is one: and you shall love the Lord your God with all your heart, and with all your soul, and with all your mind, and with all your strength' (Mark 12:29-31 and parallels).The second is this, You shall love your neighbour as yourself. There is no other commandment greater than these."

Many years ago I attempted to enter into a theological dialogue with my cousin who had gone to live in India in the early 1970s and was working as a librarian in an ashram there. He is still there now and has written a number of books on Hindu topics including translations of the work of some gurus. I asked him in a letter whether he thought that some people were naturally more able to appreciate the nature of God and were therefore more able to relate to God directly rather than needing an intermediary. (I was thinking of the Christian perspective but it might just as well apply to gurus I suppose.) To my surprise he replied in the negative and then wrote to the effect "For myself I simply try to love God with my whole being and love my neighbour as myself". I recall that he was unhappy with the idea of creation "ex nihilo", preferring by implication the presence of God in the whole creation. At the time I am not sure that I had even given the latter topic much thought but it does seem to tie in with what I have now written above. If there is no distinction between God and the creative Word/Spirit and if the divine indwells the whole of Creation then the fine point about "ex nihilo" does not seem hugely significant—not to me at least!

What was of course much more significant was that my cousin had used the words of Jesus to explain his relationship with God and the community. Like many people today he had been brought up in a Christian context but had lost patience with the demands of Christian dogma.

For seven years I was part-time chaplain at a Young Offenders Institution and Young Adults Prison. We had an ecumenical chaplaincy there which incorporated chaplaincy to the Muslim inmates, of which there were, sadly, an increasing number. To that end a Muslim chaplain, a young Imam, was appointed, firstly part-time but quite soon after in a full-time capacity. As a team we worked with all offenders administratively and pastorally other than when it became a matter of services, prayers and festivals.

Early on in this working relationship the Imam and I had a conversation about what separated Christianity and Islam. Since the Trinity is one area of contention I shared my own perspective (outlined above) with him. He had no problem with it at all. Much later on we had a visiting group of Methodists from Berlin in our area and we took them to the prison to see what prison chaplaincy in Britain involved. As part of this we visited the recently completed mosque and at the end of the visit the Imam, at our request, said a short prayer with us. He spoke it first in Arabic but then translated it into English. If you had not known it was the prayer of a Muslim you would not have recognised it as being anything other than Christian.

It is, of course, in the current climate of fear and prejudice a long way from imagining faiths working more closely together. A local Baptist colleague of mine tells how in the course of an ecumenical visit to Syria he was invited to preach at prayers in a large mosque in Damascus. Imagine that! (*Spirituality or Religion?* Gethin Abraham-Williams, p107) "In accepting the invitation to be the main Friday Sermon speaker alongside Sheikh Salah Eddin Kuftaro, in the huge Abu Nour mosque in Damascus I was agreeing, certainly tacitly, that points of contact between world faiths are at least, if not more, important than those between separate strands of the same faith". He was not without misgivings in doing this. Mind you, with his background in ecumenism Gethin would be the first to admit that it is hard enough to get on with other Christians, let alone other faiths!

So many of the world's problems, as atheists are fond of reminding us, derive from religious disputes and not a few of them within the so-called Christian family. Near to home for us in Britain, the long running "troubles" in Northern Ireland were deeply entrenched in separation and mistrust between the Catholic and Protestant communities which were exploited by both sides for political gain. The sight of Dr Ian Paisley shaking hands with the leadership of the Republican Sinn Fein party was something which many had believed would never happen. Yet within the Irish community both North and South there were Christians working ecumenically to aid reconciliation and to facilitate contact and negotiations between the two sides.

One of the roots of the mistrust between the two sides was an extreme theological stance on the part of, in particular, some Independent Presbyterians who considered the Pope to be of the Devil and the Catholic Church the "Great Whore of Babylon". I recall my shock when a young lady from Northern Ireland who was attending our church in South Wales, and who had come each Sunday to our house for lunch, exploded almost incandescently when I made what I considered a fairly mild criticism of the state of affairs in the Province. Feelings run much deeper than intellectual judgement and much of our religious context owes a great deal to our upbringing and personal life journey.

Christians will often describe Hindus as people who worship many gods, yet, notwithstanding that there certainly are many images within Hinduism, Hindus themselves would I think maintain that these images are only ways of trying to access the ineffable nature of the one divine force who holds all things in being.

When it comes to relationships between people of different faiths it becomes even more difficult because we generally define ourselves over against others. Muslims made a great play of the fact that they worshipped the only one God whilst Christians had three gods, which was idolatry. We of course recognise the error of the criticism but that makes little difference well over a thousand years later. A story repeated often enough becomes a truth. Similarly there is a widespread belief in the Islamic community that the anti-Semitic forgery *The Protocols of the Elders of Zion* is a genuine document.

It does not take much at present to convince non-Muslims that Islam is a religion of militant extremists who aim to take over the world. This despite the fact that Islam literally means "peace" and the vast majority of Muslims have no time at all for their extremist fringe.

Nevertheless it still seems to me that if the will of the Lord is that we should love our neighbour as ourselves—which Jesus of course also explained in terms of the story of the Good Samaritan—then we should put our main effort into understanding and helping one another and much less into trying to define what separates us.

The mending of relationships at the personal level and the mending of the much more significant divisions that exist within the world of faiths and international politics must be a serious objective for anyone who takes the subject of healing seriously.

6.2 Healing the Environment and the World

It is arguable that much of what follows could just as easily be written from a secular humanist perspective as from a Christian one. However my intention is to see whether a theological perspective based on the centrality of healing can offer a model with which to approach the topic.

I have to admit that I am not a green enthusiast. That is to say that while I assent too much of what is being undertaken in the name of preserving the planet I am nevertheless a bit grudging and even sometimes suspicious when policies affect me personally. Reducing our dependence on fossil fuels is sensible but I am no happier than anyone else when the petrol price goes up—not least because I run cars for a long time and the older ones are less fuel efficient. (Nor could I at present possibly afford the price of a vehicle using alternative fuels.) But then again, all is not necessarily agreed internationally. In some countries diesel engines are encouraged because they use less fuel, while in others, notably the United Kingdom, diesel fuel is taxed more highly because it is considered a pollutant.

What are we to make of the distinction between care for the environment and preserving the countryside? Whilst pursuing our policy of reducing fossil fuel dependency we are building wind turbines all over the place. Wherever they are installed people complain about them; if they are at sea they spoil the sea view from the shore; if they are on the land they spoil the view there too. Personally I find them attractive in themselves so neither argument moves me very much.

Similarly when the vast scheme to harness the tidal power of the River Severn by building a barrage from the English bank to the Welsh one was first being contemplated some twenty-five years or so ago, one of the main reasons for rejecting it was the impact it would have had on the estuary bird life. Is it brutal of me to suggest that the birds would probably move to a different location up or down stream where the mud itself had gone?

In the same vein I wonder why we want to maintain landscapes just as they are when only a few centuries ago our British mountains were wooded whereas they are now predominantly barren—the romantic would say "wild". Whilst writing these pages I have been travelling through areas of France, Germany and Austria which are heavily forested and where a large proportion of houses or their components are built using wood and wood derivatives.

Again I wonder how important it is to prevent individual species from becoming extinct. Would it really make a significant difference to the world if there were no more pandas? Is the world a poorer place for the lack of a dodo? I appreciate the argument that many plants are being lost because of heavy deforestation before we have had a chance to discover whether they might have healing properties—and you would think therefore that in the context of this book I ought to be up in arms about it. I guess it has to do with proportionality rather than hard and fast rules. The environmentalists' argument would probably be that it is better to stop all loss of habitat rather than risking any particular and potentially valuable new beneficial source.

That said I am not a climate sceptic, though I do sometimes worry that the climate change lobby overstates its case and thereby loses its moral authority. If there is a change in the Earth's temperature which could seriously affect the weather patterns and the fertility of the land in different parts of the World we would be very ill-advised to simply wait and see what happens if there are possible responses we can make to mitigate the trend and its inevitable consequences.

I wrote earlier of my agreement with Alan E Lewis in his analysis of the way forward in approaching the problems of contemporary society. He does so from the point of the paradox that God's power is fulfilled through self-emptying, "Divine *kenosis*". He writes of 'that strangely dynamic love which, because it expresses and perfects itself through self-denial and contraction, actually increases and expands the more it gives itself to opposition and negation'. Faced with the 'moribund wastelands of history's foolishness and evil' 'God's love harvest(s) a surplus of life, creativity and wholeness'.

My own model would suggest that anything, which by its effect increases integration rather than disintegration, is by definition enabling wholeness which is the final objective of the 'God whose being is in becoming'. That is of course easily said and there is undoubtedly a large measure of self-negation or self-sacrifice required if there is to be true justice in society and proper stewardship of the Earth's bountiful resources.

Alan E Lewis was writing before the traumatic events of 9/11 and the more recent collapse of the banking system, both of which have significantly redrawn many international priorities, but he made points which are still relevant.

In the 1990s a "new paradigm" accompanied the stock market bubble of the "Dotcom" era during which many people made huge fortunes at the cost of over-optimistic speculators. In the 2000s economists seem to have been convinced of the arrival of a new paradigm of continuous growth—"the end of boom and bust". The banking collapse of 2009 revealed a culture in which people thought that if bad risks were all wrapped up together they would become safe. It seems to me that anyone with a modicum of common sense could have predicted the disastrous outcome of all of these paradigms. Just because you can move money around faster it does not mean that you have any more of it. The resemblance to the party game "musical chairs" is uncanny: to begin with only one or two people are excluded but the more chairs are removed the more frantic the rush becomes until the music finally stops. In the case of the banking crisis a number of significant players fell out, quite dramatically, and in the end it was the governments and the taxpayers who stopped the music before it went too far.

The model in play is one of inequality and exploitation of people and resources. One popular rationale in economic terms was the "trickle down theory"—popular in Britain in the "Thatcher Years". This used the argument that only if you allowed people who were capable to become wealthy would resources become available to provide care for the poorest. Tony Blair apparently said he was comfortable with some people being very wealthy—presumably because they were generating wealth for the whole economy. There is no doubting that the average household income for most people in Britain and most developed countries did in fact increase over the last few decades but there is still a stubbornly high number of people left behind at the bottom of the heap and what is more because of the need for multiple income families many people's actual standard of living or well-being has not increased. Levels of stress and dislocation have certainly increased.

When Jesus spoke about wealth he did so in a way which was challenging for his hearers then and it remains so today. "How hard if will be for a rich man to enter the Kingdom of Heaven"; "Go, sell all you have, give it to the poor and come and follow me"; the story of Dives and Lazarus—the rich man who ignored the beggar at his door; the commendation of the widow's small but sacrificial contribution to the temple coffers; the farmer who had a bumper harvest and built bigger barns. When he sent his disciples out on mission he told them not to take extra clothing and provisions with them but to depend on generosity (a better bet in middle eastern society even today than in our well-to-do welfare states). The precarious nature of financial assets was illustrated in the story of the Lost Son who was popular as long as he had money but was dropped the moment it ran out.

The difficult thing is that we are all enmeshed in a system from which it is extremely difficult to escape. For decades our housing and transport policies have encouraged people to commute large distances to work. Inevitably they have to buy and run cars which necessitate new roads and consume oil products. We have allowed, and benefited financially from, the concentration of retail selling in supermarkets which has in turn undermined the trade of small businesses in town and village centres. In the United States it is almost unthinkable that you could exist without a car—my wife and I were nearly picked up by the police there because we were walking down a (perfectly respectable!) residential street. (A friend told us of a neighbour who used to get in the car to drive to her letter box at the bottom of the drive but I think that was a bit extreme!) If you base your whole lifestyle around vehicles it is then extremely difficult suddenly to adjust to an increase in the cost of fuel.

I do not write this with any sense of personal complacency. The fact that I have worked abroad means that we have a network of close friendships and family relationships which, if we are to maintain them, necessitate travelling significant distances. This would never have happened in an age when people rarely moved far beyond their birth community.

When we look at the consequences of climate change we notice that most of the people severely affected will be in poorer and marginal countries. Some Pacific islands will disappear completely. Lands which are subject to flooding now are likely to have even more inundation and may become uninhabitable. Some areas are going to become arid. Of course, some areas will benefit from a warmer climate. But there will undoubtedly be consequences in terms of population movement and the need to accept refugees from places where life is no longer sustainable. There are likely to be conflicts over water resources, especially where rivers flow through several countries. Unless we are going to shut people out and leave them to their own fate we are going to have to come to terms with it as our own problem too and then see what can be done.

The truth is that we face two genuine options. We can continue to "go for growth" which will inevitably lead either to the exploitation and degradation of the environment and/or to the increasing exploitation of producers, or we can gradually accept lower standards of living, concentrating on maintaining the qualities that are genuinely life-enhancing and starting to do without those things which we do not genuinely need. That includes willingness to share our space when migration becomes necessary.

Alan E Lewis wrote of self-emptying. It seems to me that we have to be prepared to do just that. In the life of Jesus portrayed in the Gospels we see a man who accepted God's priorities as his own and took the consequences. It meant that when he acted in accordance with those priorities he came into conflict with the authorities—for the most part the religious ones. The Jewish scriptures make it clear that God is more interested in the welfare of the marginalised than in "authentic" or correct religious ritual. A "godly" society is going to be one in which the weak and the marginalised are strengthened and drawn in, valued for who they are and not judged on the basis of their condition or circumstances.

The way in which people with physical or mental incapacity are integrated into British society today is a positive example, though I suspect that there is much more we could do. The same could be said of attitudes to people of different nationality and ethnic origin, and of sexual orientation. The sad thing is that we have required legislation to achieve this positive development. And a lot of underlying animosity still exists which would quickly resurface given half a chance. Ultimately change has to come from within.

In discussing healing of the individual it was suggested that a relationship of love was necessary. All our policies and their implementation need to be underpinned by an attitude of love — that is defined by a desire for all concerned to be completely fulfilled. When it comes to the environment reciprocal love is somewhat problematic but nevertheless any concerns for the environment have ultimately to be grounded in a recognition that the finite resources of the world are a blessing which should not be squandered, abused or indeed hoarded for personal or factional gain.

It has to be admitted that it is hard enough dealing with these issues at the personal level let alone at a societal or international one, but the difficulty should not be allowed to be an excuse. Underlying all the difficulties are deep-seated human needs and habits of thought which lead to suspicion of "others" and a desire for defined boundaries. The "boundaries" may be physical ones—garden fences, national border crossings—or they may be in the mind. Living as a foreigner in another country alters your perceptions significantly. I suspect I might always have said that as a Christian I had more in common with other Christians than with many other people with whom I shared British Citizenship. Living in Berlin and having German friends and neighbours, as well as working in an international congregation, it became absolutely clear that I had more in common with the people who shared my particular strand of faith than with anyone else at all. I was still exhilarated when England for once beat Germany at football—there is a residue in all of us!— but I would have welcomed the introduction of the Euro as a British currency. (Whether it would have been a good thing at the time I now doubt, as it happens, especially bearing in mind the crisis which resulted from the disparities between the different economies in the Euro-zone.)

Nevertheless, for all the breaking down of boundaries in my own life, there are still plenty more that need addressing, and some of them, if I am to do so will undoubtedly be painful. This is the point at which the theological ideal starts to look unattainable. Jesus said 'Be perfect, as your heavenly Father is perfect', with the implicit idea of "becoming", of progressing, of moving onward towards a target.

When, as most church-goers do most weeks, we pray for the peace of the world, or reconciliation between Jew and Palestinian, do we actually expect God to intervene, knock a few heads together so that peace will break out? I doubt it. Some people actually do something by getting involved. Others support them financially. It may be a cliché that God has no hands but ours but it no less true for all that. That God restricts that use of hands to confessing Christians is I suspect less true. Or take the frequently used example of Mahatma Gandhi, who through his leadership of non-violent protest contributed to huge change in India. He admitted to being a follower of the teaching of Christ but was wittily scathing about the ability of Christians to do the same! I have no doubt in my mind that Gandhi was fully in tune with mind of God (the Logos) and that he therefore acted in a way which was godly. That does not mean he was always right, but few would deny him the designation "saintly".

I was deeply moved by the Nobel Laureate Aung San Suu

Kyi's first 2011 Reith Lecture in which she addressed the subject of liberty. She spoke about personal freedom and spiritual freedom within the context of her own engagement with Burmese politics. What was impressive was the extent to which she drew on her Buddhist background but was noticeably also implicitly drawing on Christian tradition for her illustrations. We have a tendency as Christians to criticise Buddhism because of its focus on freedom from desire which suggests for us a lack of engagement with worldly concerns. These are her own words: "when the Buddhist monks of Burma went on a Metta—that is loving kindness—march in 2007, they were protesting against the sudden steep rise in the price of fuel that had led to a devastating rise in food prices. They were using the spiritual authority to move for the basic right of the people to affordable food." I would want to suggest that in doing so they were allying themselves with the continuing healing work of God in the world.

When President Obama, in the first flush of his presidency, made a priority to reach out to the Muslim world it was recognised by a, some think premature, award of the Nobel Peace Prize. Premature or not, I found it a wholly laudable attempt to break through the barriers of antagonism and suspicion which have dogged world relations for too long. It will be some time yet before we see the results, though the changing political landscape in the Middle East may contribute.

In an earlier chapter I quoted Frances Young's address to an interfaith event in Doha. That Islamic and Christian scholars can meet and share perspectives, seeking to find common ground, is another sign of hope. We need to find ways to support and encourage those who join together in such ventures, especially those at a local level where mutual understanding can be very productive in improving community relations. This of course applies within faith communities too, where divisions are often deeper than with those "outside".

I have a suspicion that anyone approaching issues of this nature from a religious perspective is going to end up with a similar commentary on the ills of society and in all probability a similar prescription. Some will undoubtedly observe that if you draw the boundaries of healing as widely as this it encompasses everything and perhaps therefore becomes almost meaningless. Nevertheless I want to maintain my conviction that all our activities should be directed towards enabling others to reach the potential which God intends, which is true wholeness.

If this seems to have reduced or watered down healing I want to use the final chapter to suggest a model of Church as Therapeutic Community and in doing so, though I will use a particular example to illustrate what I mean, I would want to encourage the Church—and therefore each local church community—to review its life and activities in the light of Jesus' instruction to preach and to heal.

Chapter 7

Church as Therapeutic Community

The quotations that follow are representative of the focus of the contemporary Methodist Church in Britain. The local one could be from any number of local contexts. The others reflect far more the overview of Methodism. In my opinion, any reference to healing is at best obtuse. I suspect the same would apply if I invited contributions from other denominations.

A local Methodist Church:

****** Methodist Church exists to share with all
The glory of God through worship
The love of God through service and
The Spirit of God through friendship.

The Methodist Church in Britain describes its priority thus:

"To proclaim and affirm its conviction of God's love in Christ, for us and for all the world; and renew confidence in God's presence and action in the world and in the church."

The Wales Synod of the Methodist Church states:

"We exist to support God's mission and the ministry of the Methodist Church.

We encourage and enable the developments of Circuits, local Churches and individuals to engage more effectively in worship, learning, caring, service and evangelism."

The Birmingham Methodist District states:

"Our Priority is Mission. In attending to this, the essence of our faith, we have created new circuits, each shaped to meet our calling to worship, witness, sharing and service. We seek to do everything in partnership with Christians and others in local communities, in a global perspective."

In Luke 9:2 Jesus sends out his disciples "to preach the kingdom of God and to heal the sick" and in verse 6 "they departed, and went throughout the villages, preaching the gospel, and healing everywhere."

In Mark 1:15 we are told that Jesus challenged his hearers to respond to the presence of the Kingdom of God by repenting and receiving the good news.

My personal frustration is that our identification of proclamation as a priority is clear but the parallel strand of healing is not mentioned at all!

I guess my personal "mission statement" would have to be "To declare God's loving acceptance of all people and to express it through a healing presence in the world." I would hope that is consistent with the biblical references above.

Does it matter how it is expressed if the actions of the church community are implicitly linked to the wider definition of healing? Well actually I think it does and I will seek to show how it might look if we took such a perspective seriously. In the next three sections I will draw on the principles and practice of Parish Nursing, though it has to be said that I have my own particular "slant" on how they should be applied.

It needs to be stressed here—taking into account the numerical strength/weakness of most local churches—that although this refers to individual churches it could just as well apply to a group of churches working together within a denomination or ecumenically.

7.1 The "Health Cabinet"

I have to admit that this term still makes me smile. It is not a medicine cupboard but a committee or working group of a local church whose brief is to consider the mission of that local church with respect to matters related to health and wholeness. It is a term I met when first reading about Parish Nursing (see next section).

The idea, as I understand it, is to bring together a group of people with expertise in medical and pastoral care and invite them to review all aspects of the life of the local church as they impinge on health and well-being. The sort of people involved, apart from the clergy team, could be health professionals such as doctors, nurses, physiotherapists, occupational therapists, dentists, social workers, pastoral visitors, alternative health therapists etc.

If we accept the premise that we have a responsibility for health promotion as well as for caring for the sick then aspects of outreach to those who are marginalised would form part of the agenda, as would the encouragement of teaching and training in health issues as part of the group activities of the church. The group would be able to provide training for those engaged in pastoral visiting to equip them with appropriate skills. They would also presumably be able to highlight activities or areas which were not health-enhancing.

The overall intention is to ensure that health and wholeness has a central and a focussed presence in the life of the local church. The Cabinet would meet on a regular basis — though that might only be once a year — and would have a formal input to the local church's main decision-making body.

7.2 Parish Nursing

As I indicated above I first met the "Health Cabinet" whilst reading about Parish Nursing. The term "Parish Nursing" relates to a form of pastoral care which has now been practised in the

United States for decades and is thus familiar there. There are also Parish Nurses in Canada and New Zealand (at least) but they are still a comparative rarity in the United Kingdom. The trouble is that neither term is actually accurate since "Parish" has a different connotation in the UK—either politically or denominationally—and "Nursing" implies a registered status within the profession. Having said that, I will continue to use the term for the moment.

In trying to explain the concept of Parish Nursing I tend to describe it as "pastoral care enhanced by medical expertise and a concern for spiritual well-being". If you would like an alternative and much more thorough description I would refer you to the website of Parish Nursing Ministries UK (www.parishnursing .org.uk). This organisation restricts its definition to "registered nurses" which I consider is actually too narrow a definition for the work that can be carried out under this general heading. Nevertheless I commend their work and would encourage further contact with them for those who may be interested.

In the next section I will outline a specific pilot project with which I was engaged but here I will give other examples. In the introduction (p6) I referred to a study visit to Holland, Michigan in the course of which I was able to meet with and explore the work of a number of Parish Nurses. There were two models of operation in that community. Because of matters of employment a group of churches appointed Parish Nurses through the local community hospital. When I met her the coordinator of this group of nurses was in the course of writing a review of their work to indicate to the hospital what the value of this contribution was. It was good to hear subsequently that the review had been favourably received and that the working relationship continued.

I had thought that a model based on health care in the United States probably would not transfer because of the difference in the systems but actually there were enough similarities to encourage some sort of developments here.

For example, a Parish Nurse in the local United Methodist Church had recently organised a "Brown Bag Day" on which members of the community could bring their medications to the church, where they could discuss them with a group of pharmacists. This same nurse had, through a pastoral contact, become involved in developing a bank of bone marrow donors in the local community. Neither of these initiatives was restricted to the church congregation. Her regular weekly engagement was to take blood pressure for members of the congregation after the morning worship. (Apparently this is a good time to do so because they will have been sitting and relaxing for an hour or so—obviously not hell-fire preaching then!) She had also produced a liturgy for the "Blessing of Hands" which was offered to staff in the local hospital and apparently much appreciated.

The Parish Nurse in the church where my hosts worshipped was not one of the groups associated with the hospital. She worked half-time and did so alongside the Pastor and occasionally a visiting Deaconess. It has to be said that there was some confusion there over division of duties and responsibilities. However she also offered a weekly class on health issues. I visited this one week and the topic was nutrition. I found it a very helpful session. She was a qualified nurse whose office shelves were well stocked with medical and health books.

Neither of these two did what most people tend to identify with "nursing". They did not get involved with the administration of medicines or treatments beyond taking blood pressure. Rather they were engaged in health promotion and also monitoring within a context of pastoral care.

Nevertheless even such a restricted application of "nursing" gives a good indication as to what might be adopted in Britain. How many local churches offer such things as part of their programme?

7.3 Parish Nursing Pilot Project—Lichfield

On my return from my sabbatical visit to Holland, Michigan, in 2003 I was convinced that this was a model worth pursuing for implementation in the UK. I was fortunate (blessed?) in having a local church willing to support such a venture, including a particular individual who had the skills and qualifications, and in due course the support of the Birmingham District and the Methodist Church Connexional Priority Fund so that we were able to make a full-time appointment for up to five years. As it transpired the person appointed was unable to complete the full period because of her own ill health but the results of the pilot gave clear indications of the opportunities as well as the limitations in such an appointment.

The objective of the study was to establish whether the promotion of health and wholeness is a valid ministry of the church and if so whether the Parish Nursing model is the most appropriate. The person appointed worked initially in a part-time voluntary capacity and undertook training through Parish Nursing Ministries UK. When the appointment became paid and full-time it was envisaged that 50% of the time would be dedicated to the research and to promotional activities. In the event the pastoral load rapidly took a dominant proportion of her time. Nevertheless a formal evaluation was possible by an independent agency which gave clear indications of the scope and possibilities of such a scheme.

In the course of the study, for reasons discussed above, the title changed but when the post was finally re-advertised it was designated: Pastoral Worker – Health and Wholeness (Parish Nurse)—which doesn't exactly trip of the tongue but is accurate enough! I will, despite what I said, nevertheless use "Parish Nurse" as a shorthand term below.

Initially one might ask how much potential work there might be for such a person, but the way the workload developed in the first few months made it emphatically clear that here was work to be done, which was not otherwise being covered. The best way to deal with it is to use actual examples. For the most part, no names or different names are used so as to protect the identities of the people concerned.

Even before we had appointed a Parish Nurse we had a conversation in our Pastoral Committee regarding an elderly couple over whose health circumstances we were unhappy. One partner had had a stroke and was unable to speak properly though otherwise mentally competent; the other, who was the carer, was showing signs of dementia, but these were well disguised and the family had not noticed. We felt powerless to act. In the event things came to a head shortly after the Parish Nurse had been formally appointed. The carer had to be admitted urgently to hospital. The partner was taken to the hospital by friends but was then unable to communicate with the hospital staff. The Parish Nurse contacted the family, who were not local, indicating the seriousness of the position, and the local care team. She then arranged with another church member to stay the night with the partner who needed care. Clearly without the particular knowledge and expertise we, the church community, would have been much less able to give support.

I know this to be the case because when my own mother was found in a very poorly state we brought her back to our home where we called the Parish Nurse. She examined her and immediately called the local GP insisting that she be seen immediately. My mother's local church could not have offered any support to her or to us as a family, not because they didn't care but because they had no agenda to do so nor people in a position to respond.

As an indication of the difference it makes having medical concerns on the pastoral agenda: at a meeting a couple of years later we responded very quickly to concerns about someone who was clearly developing dementia but whose partner was still permitting them to drive the car. We contemplated contacting the family doctor, but in the end I was delegated to talk to the son-in-law about it. He was relieved that someone outside the family circle had raised the matter.

Sometimes the support that is needed may appear very trivial but can be none the less significant. Such a case would be the young mother who needed to go to the dentist but had a phobia about dentists' surgeries. A member of the parish nursing team, a retired dentist, offered to go with her. That was all the support she needed.

I have just added "the parish nursing team" to the narrative. One of the Parish Nurse's responsibilities was to recruit volunteers to assist in the cases which were referred to her. This she did. The team included others who had had nursing experience as well as pastoral visitors who were suitable. In general, if such a scheme is to be introduced it is essential that appropriate training be given to those concerned.

As the average age of congregations rises there are increasingly issues of, on the one hand, supporting couples where one has become a carer and, on the other hand, supporting those who are alone.

As an example of the latter, and again from direct personal experience: my mother, then about 81 years old, was still driving her car and lived in what had been her home area since childhood. She had a consultant appointment at the local hospital. I was unable to go with her and encouraged her to go by herself but she insisted on a friend taking her. I am of course open to accusation of insensitivity but it resulted in her saying that she just wanted someone with her when she went to the specialist. Within the Parish Nursing scheme accompaniment or advocacy was offered if people needed it. With hindsight I can say that it is often those who are closest to people who fail to notice their deterioration.

From the point of view of home support, there are many Live at Home schemes around the country. The "Methodist Homes for the Aged, Live at Home Scheme" was originally piloted at Lichfield too. Clearly it is pointless to duplicate what is being offered by another agency but I would suggest that if such a scheme operates within the aegis of a local church then it ought to be incorporated into the pastoral oversight in some way or other and certainly have a recognised relationship with any parish nursing scheme.

One of the most difficult areas of pastoral care is helping people to face terminal illness. The information from medical services and also from support networks is usually very good but time is always limited and it can be helpful to have someone else to offer support who has themselves, or has access to, medical expertise. I can recall four cases within two years where the support of the parish nursing team was appreciated in different ways. In one case the one partner was suffering with early onset dementia whilst the carer was subject to a tumour on the spine. Pastoral support was given by a team and help and advice was given by the Parish Nurse. In another case one partner had cancer and the other partner was depressive. In another an active member was struggling with bowel cancer which had been in remission. In a fourth case the Parish Nurse, at no little cost to her own position and the status of the project, intervened to get a member out of hospital and into hospice care when the hospital care was clearly inadequate. She then accompanied the partner in dealing with a complaint to the hospital about inadequate care.

In a different situation there was a difficult context where the couple, who were very long-standing members of the church and generally well cared for, wanted the church to provide support beyond what was reasonable for volunteers. The skills of the parish nursing team were very much needed to persuade them that professional help was necessary.

In all these circumstances the extra contribution which is brought is a spiritual dimension. It is essential that the one offering care does so with recognition of the value of prayerful support and almost certainly with strength of personal conviction, faith and spirituality too. It is not a matter of completing an academic course and applying the facts.

One of the other things that a Parish Nurse can offer is time. So often the provision of care in the health sector is constrained by an appointment system or simply by sheer pressure of numbers. I recall when I was a hospital chaplain having a conversation over lunch with one of the consultant orthopaedic surgeons. His observation, which took me by surprise, since I was really trying to see if we could integrate laying-on of hands into pain relief, was that many of the patients who came to see him suffering back pain would benefit more from twenty minutes spent with someone like me, and he was not speaking of spiritual healing. It was simply that much back pain is the result of stress and the solution is more likely to be talking therapy than surgery.

As volunteers we can be much more generous with our time. Another personal example: My wife has had various physical problems over many years, often leading to depression. She was at a particularly low ebb at one point, and I took her to see the Parish Nurse. I recall she was so low that she actually went wearing her dressing gown. In the hour that followed the two of them reviewed her whole medical history and came to the conclusion that she had a different condition altogether that was showing through these symptoms. The consequence was an appointment with the family doctor, to which the Parish Nurse accompanied her, as a result of which a completely new course of action and treatment followed. A pity there had not been more time in the statutory system years earlier!

One of the interesting features of having a designated person for health and wholeness in the church is that they become a first port of call for people who really do not know whether they ought to bother their doctor with some minor condition or complaint. They also offer a service which is based, at least some of the time, on non-medical premises. Furthermore, especially if the church is open to the public through such services as a coffee shop, it is possible for non-church people to access assistance too.

This has all had to do with people already suffering illness in some way or another. But much was made earlier of the importance of health promotion. Specific courses were offered through the auspices of St John Ambulance and Epilepsy Action. There was a Parish Nursing Notice Board in a public area which was regularly updated. When I left Lichfield in 2009 a team had agreed to put a different display on the board each month.

It was proposed, but at the time not yet implemented, that each group meeting within the church community should be asked to have at least one health related topic in their annual programme of activities.

I recall a vain attempt to mitigate the offering of cakes in the coffee shop by providing fruit as a healthy alternative. Unfortunately the public were not particularly responsive. However the leaders in the parent and toddler group agreed early on that the snacks for the children should be healthy ones.

If there is an ongoing pattern of healing services in the local church it would be sensible for the Parish Nurse to be involved in them. In the case of Lichfield the person concerned was one of several who completed a short training course which I led. She, along with the others shared in the laying-on of hands in the monthly healing service.

I hinted earlier that it was not always easy to work alongside the statutory sector. Despite being a registered nurse the Parish Nurse was unable to access information in any way different from any other member of the public. And when we tried to develop cooperation with the Primary Care Trust they insisted that, although they recognised what we were offering as positive and helpful, we could only work with them if we had a formal contractual relationship. This would of course mean more bureaucracy. On the same lines it became clear that the paperwork necessary to maintain the Parish Nurse's registered status was out of all proportion to the benefit gained. For this reason I am convinced that as long as the person carrying out this health and wholeness function in the local church is professionally trained and experienced in health care and has previously been in good standing with their professional body, they should be able to be appointed. If they are successful in drawing together a team of volunteers, the chances are that any deficiencies in skill and experience will be compensated by those of another member of the team.

At the last meeting of the equivalent of the Health Cabinet at Lichfield before I left there were three active community nurses, a retired dentist, a physiotherapist, an occupational therapist, and three retired nurses, one of whom was fulfilling the role of coordinator. Within the congregation there was a retired local GP and a consultant paediatrician.

From all that I have written you will gather that this was a fairly large church community. The membership was about 280. There was also a good range of ages. As I suggested earlier, the majority of churches today are much smaller in terms of membership and are likely to have a much smaller pool of professional skills and experience. But that should not be grounds for dismissing the concept.

In the proposals for the pilot study we had always foreseen the possibility of working ecumenically with the neighbouring churches to provide a wider team of people and expertise. From a British Methodist point of view that could be done on a Circuit basis. There are also a number of members of the Methodist Diaconal Order who have nursing qualifications. I believe it could be seen as an appropriate use of their previous experience to place them in appointments in churches or contexts which might be focussed on health and wholeness. Other denominations have similar local structures and experienced health professionals within their ministry teams to enable equivalent schemes to be implemented.

7.4 Conclusion

Despite the case that there are occasionally dysfunctional church communities, just as there are dysfunctional families, the majority of the churches that I have come across are actually actively caring institutions within whose compass there are many individuals who, whether they appreciate it or not, are engaged in healing ministry. In an age in which public money is going to continue to be tight, and at a time when the proportion of elderly in the population is increasing, with all that this implies, it does not require a great deal of imagination to see how the church can engage with its own community and that of the wider society to offer care which is enriched by a commitment born of a faith, whose founder and continuing source of inspiration and power made a central focus of his ministry loving concern for those who were excluded from society, and especially the sick.

I would offer the Parish Nursing model as one which is worthy of consideration but would even more so recommend that local churches assess their healing ministry, using the far wider definition which I have proposed in the course of this book. It would hopefully become focussed and be publicly affirmed rather than diffused and unmonitored and would become central to the worship and pastoral life of the church.

As a Superintendent minister I am only too well aware how agendas can become a burden to ministers and members alike but I would nevertheless encourage the inclusion of an item in the agendas of their Church Council or their equivalent to review what that particular local church is doing to respond to Jesus' commission to preach and to heal.

Chapter 8

Postscript

In the course of writing this I have tried to deal with some of the issues which confront anyone working within the area of healing. Those who do so are inevitably faced with such questions as the cause of suffering; why God appears to intervene in some cases and not in others; why people who are prayed for with great faith and conviction die; why some people have gifts and others not.

I have tried to reflect out of the reality of my own personal experience, in the light of the Bible and in particular the definitive example of Jesus. I have questioned traditional understandings where these seem to detract from a full appreciation of the way God seems to work in practice.

This leads to my conviction that healing, in whatever form it is considered, is the result of our coming into conformity with the developing providence of God. It is, I believe, God's purpose that all people, and indeed the whole Creation—physical and spiritual—become the best that they can be; that they be fulfilled. Anything which we can do to enable this is godly work. In fact it is a continuation of the Incarnation of God which was expressed in the person and ministry of Jesus.

If we take this seriously as individuals and as the Christian community, it will define the way we live our lives and how we relate to the society at large. I am convinced that this can best be enabled by having a positive agenda for health and wholeness within the church at every level and especially at the level of governance.

I have given one example of how this can be put into practice in a local church setting. I do not pretend that this is the only way to do so but from conversations with individuals, charities and government agencies in the area of my current appointment it is clear that such initiatives would be welcomed and supported if the church took the lead.

One such proposal could see an ageing traditional building being replaced by a community facility which focussed its outreach on health and wholeness for the local area.

I am sure that this model of "Church as Therapeutic Community" can be used to facilitate reconciliation within and between human societies and cultures. It would not necessarily be new work—it already happens in many places, such as Northern Ireland and Israel/Palestine, though I suspect that few of those doing the work have defined it as a "ministry of healing".

Similarly any activity which seeks to overcome injustice and to integrate the marginalised, or to work for a more sustainable and fair distribution of the world's resources is one which also has a healing dimension.

Meanwhile I continue to offer healing on a personal basis as and when the opportunity presents itself. I would encourage everyone to follow through on the implications of the proposal that healing is part of the natural (God-created) order and not the result of God stepping in to overrule the natural laws.

I was amazed to discover that I had this ability to heal. I am convinced that rather than seeing this as a special "gift" we should learn to perceive it as a "given" of human existence.

Clearly some people, as with other "givens" like musical ability, will be able to develop more competence than others, and the longer we perform and practice anything the more perceptive we generally become.

If this is an innate ability, which is what I am suggesting, how much more will it achieve when anchored in the reality of a faith which expresses itself most fully in the operation of self-giving love?

Bibliography

"Alive and Kicking" by Stephen Pattison (© Stephen Pattison 1989, SCM Press)

"Between Cross and Resurrection—A Theology for Holy Saturday" Alan E Lewis (© 2001, Wm B Eerdmans Publishing Co.)

"Between Heaven and Earth" by Robert A. Orsi (© 2005, Princeton University Press)

"Das Geheimnis der Heilung: Wie altes Wissen die Medizin verändert" by Joachim Faulstich (© 2010, MensSana bei Knaur-Verlag). The ARD television programme quoted in the text was based on this book.

"Healing in the New Testament" by John Pilch (© 2000, Augsburg Fortress)

"History of the Christian Church" by Philip Schaff (1910, Charles Scribner's Sons) (accessed via Database © 2004, WORDsearch Corp.)

"My Stroke of Insight" by Jill Bolte Taylor (© 2009, Hodder and Stoughton)

"Mystik und Widerstand" by Dorothee Sölle (© 1997, Hoffmann und Campe Verlag); published in English as "The Silent Cry—Mysticism and Resistance" (© 2001, Augsburg Fortress Press)

"On Christian Theology" by Rowan Williams (© 2000, Blackwell Publishing)

"Prayers and Ideas for Healing Services" by Ian Cowie (© 1995, Wild Goose Publications)

"Scriptures in Dialogue" ed. Michael Ipgrave (© 2004, Church House Publishing)

"Spirituality or Religion?" by Gethin Abraham-Williams (© 2008, O-Books)

"Why Zebras don't get Ulcers" by Robert M Sapolsky (© 2004, Holt Paperbacks)

Questions for group discussion

1. Why do we tend to think of healing as referring to physical cure? Share with the group your own experiences of how healing has led to a greater sense of wholeness of life.

2. Does our thinking about the gospel change at all if we think of salvation as healing?

3. Does thinking about the understanding of health and disease in New Testament times change the way we interpret the stories today?

4. How are the gifts of the Spirit, in respect of healing, to be exercised in the Church? How can Paul's understanding of the Church as the Body of Christ help us in this regard?

5. We tend to call "miracle" what we cannot explain in any way other than by the hand of God. Have there been experiences in your life you would call "miracle" and, if so, why?

6. Do we all have an innate capacity to heal ourselves and others? If so, why do we offer prayers to God for healing? Does prayer in some way release that capacity to heal, or does it simply enable God to bring healing into people's lives and situations?

7. In what respect would blessing a new airport make a difference to its working?

8. a. What is distinctive about Christian healing?
   b. What is meant by offering healing "in the name of Jesus"?

9. How do you respond to the idea of "prayer as body language" — prayer as action?

10. Paul says that "God was pleased to reconcile all things, whether on earth or in heaven", through Christ (Colossians 1 v. 20). As Paul also says that we share in this ministry of reconciliation (2 Corinthians 5 vv 18 & 19), how do you understand that for yourself?

11. What signs of healing or reconciling do you see in your community, in the world and in the whole created order?

12. To what extent do health and wholeness have a "central and focussed presence" in your local church or community?

13. What might be done to enable that to happen?

14. How does the example of the Parish Nursing Project help in this regard?

15. Do you think it would be correct to describe your church as a "therapeutic community"? Should it be?

Circle Books

Circle is a symbol of infinity and unity. It's part of a growing list of imprints, including o-books.net and zero-books.net.

Circle Books aims to publish books in Christian spirituality that are fresh, accessible, and stimulating.

Our books are available in all good English language bookstores worldwide. If you can't find the book on the shelves, then ask your bookstore to order it for you, quoting the ISBN and title. Or, you can order online—all major online retail sites carry our titles.

To see our list of titles, please view www.Circle-Books.com, growing by 80 titles per year.

Authors can learn more about our proposal process by going to our website and clicking on Your Company > Submissions.

We define Christian spirituality as the relationship between the self and its sense of the transcendent or sacred, which issues in literary and artistic expression, community, social activism, and practices. A wide range of disciplines within the field of religious studies can be called upon, including history, narrative studies, philosophy, theology, sociology, and psychology. Interfaith in approach, Circle Books fosters creative dialogue with non-Christian traditions.

And tune into MySpiritRadio.com for our book review radio show, hosted by June-Elleni Laine, where you can listen to authors discussing their books.

MySpiritRadio